First Year Law Student

WISDOM, WARNINGS, AND WHAT
I WISH I'D KNOWN IN MY YEAR
AS A ONE L

EDITED BY

Steven Marietti and Tammi Rice

D1431283

PUBLISHING

New York

This publication is designed to provide accurate and authoritative information in regard to the subject matter covered. It is sold with the understanding that the publisher is not engaged in rendering legal, accounting, or other professional service. If legal advice or other expert assistance is required, the services of a competent professional should be sought.

Vice President and Publisher: Maureen McMahon
Editorial Director: Jennifer Farthing
Contributing Editor: Monica Lugo
Development Editor: Andy Jacknick
Production Editor: Dominique Polfliet
Typesetter: Susan Ramundo
Cover Designer: Carly Schnur

Published by Kaplan Publishing, a division of Kaplan, Inc.
1 Liberty Plaza, 24th Floor
New York, NY 10006

Printed in the United States of America

January 2008
10 9 8 7 6 5 4 3 2 1

ISBN-13: 978-1-4277-9679-0

Kaplan Publishing books are available at special quantity discounts to use for sales promotions, employee premiums, or educational purposes. Please email our Special Sales Department to order or for more information at kaplanpublishing@kaplan.com, or write to Kaplan Publishing, 1 Liberty Plaza, 24th Floor, New York, NY 10006.

Contents

Introduction

Aristotle said that the law is reason free from passion.

But passion is something you are going to need a lot of to get through law school, and it's going to test your reason. The intense, demanding nature of law school—and the first year in particular—has been well-documented in popular culture, from Scott Turow's book *1L* about his experiences at Harvard Law, to movies like *The Paper Chase* and the recent blockbuster hit *Legally Blonde*. This is because the first year of law school is a critical time—the environment is new and the learning curve is steep.

This book is designed to help you survive—and even thrive—during your first year in law school, both inside and outside the classroom. The tales within these pages are sure to provide the support and advice that all 1Ls need.

Within these pages you'll find everything from down-to-earth humor to frank insights about maintaining motivation and practical tips that will make your life a whole lot easier. It's filled with hundreds of personal stories and advice from those who have been there and done that—who've soldiered through the Socratic method, the study groups, the summer internships—and made it through to the other side.

And so will you. Welcome to the ranks.

About the Editors

Steven Marietti is the Director of Pre-Law Programs for Kaplan Test Prep and Admissions, overseeing the development and delivery of Kaplan's national pre-law offerings. Widely cited as an expert on the LSAT and law school admissions, Steven serves as a Kaplan spokesperson on related issues and has been quoted in numerous publications nationwide. He has also appeared as a guest speaker at hundreds of universities. Steven holds a JD and an MBA from Rutgers University, and is a member of the New Jersey Bar.

Tammi Rice is the Vice President of Field Operations, Marketing, and Sales for Kaplan PMBR, overseeing the delivery of Kaplan PMBR's bar review courses nationwide. As an 18-year veteran of the education industry and a former LSAT instructor, Tammi has spoken extensively on law school admissions topics at numerous forums across the U.S. Tammi holds a JD from the University of Tulsa and also attended Southern Methodist University School of Law. She is a member of the Texas Bar.

CHAPTER 1

The Reality Check

> *"A fascination with the mechanics of the legal system and the ramifications that every legal decision has on politics, life, and even economics was the driving factor in choosing my profession."*
> —**Law Student, San Francisco, CA**

Congratulations! You are about to enter a profession that will create innumerable opportunities for you. It is an education and experience like no other.

On the pages that follow, the Voices of Experience will weigh in on what it is like to take this step. You will probably hear from them a number of things you have been curious or concerned about. You will also get an advanced look at some of the surprises—both good and challenging—that go with the territory. Learning to be a lawyer can be very rewarding, but no one (or very few) will say that it is not also challenging. The best thing is to be prepared. So read on to get ready for what is in store.

SO YOU WANT TO BE A LAWYER?

There are many reasons people decide to become lawyers. One of the great advantages of law school is that one can enter with almost any background and emerge three years later, pass the bar exam, and begin practicing law. The quotes on the next few pages, however, should give you an idea as to why the Voices of Experience chose to attend law school. In it, you'll probably find that you are not alone in your reasons for wanting to do the same!

Desire to Be in the Profession

"As long as I can remember, I've always wanted to be a lawyer."
–Law Student, St. Louis, MO

"I always had an interest in going to law school but I wanted to take some time to work in the legal field first to be sure that I wanted to make such an investment. After that, it was clear that law school was the next step in advancing my career."
–Law Student, Baltimore, MD

"I was very interested in the criminal justice field and wanted to continue my education."
–Lawyer–Criminal Law, Ipswich, MA

❝ *When I was a senior in high school, when we got to the chapter on Article III, our government teacher assigned each of us a Supreme Court case. We each had to prepare a case brief, present it to the class, and afterward we argued about the issue presented in each case. I had* Gideon v. Wainwright. *I decided then that I wanted to be a lawyer. Reading those cases (mostly from the Warren court) interested me more than anything else I had ever learned about in school.* ❞

–Law Student, New York, NY

❝ *Many people in undergrad said, 'You should go to law school if you like to argue.' Once in law school, a professor made a great point, the question is not whether you are good at arguing or you like to argue, it's do you win when you argue? That's what you look for in a lawyer—can you convince someone to change the way they think?* ❞

–Law Student, Chicago, IL

"*It was always my dream to go to law school. I reached a point in my life when I had to decide either to go to law school now or close that door forever.*"

–Lawyer–Civil Rights Law, Middletown, RI

Employment Prospects

"*I was tired of my job and the income ceiling that exists with a bachelor's degree.*"

–Law Student, San Diego, CA

"*Global outsourcing. My career in IT died the day people 14,000 miles away could securely connect to the network where I was hard-plugged in.*"

–Law Student, Los Angeles, CA

"*I wanted to go to the FBI.*"

–Lawyer–Criminal Law, Los Angeles, CA

"I was not sure what I wanted to do after college and a law degree seemed like an option that could open a lot of doors, even those outside of the traditional law realm."

–Lawyer–Class Action Law, Los Angeles, CA

"My undergrad degree (psychology) had limited career prospects. I wanted a career that had upward potential and a higher salary range. I attended law school when I did so that I could become an attorney while I was still young and could make a lifelong career out of it, and before I forgot how to study hard."

–Law Student, Houston, TX

"Because I majored in political science and Spanish, which only goes so far."

–Law Student, New Orleans, LA

"Because this is a profession that gives you freedom."

–Lawyer–Bankruptcy Law, Brooklyn, NY

To Gain Valuable Skills

"I have always seen a legal education as excellent preparation for almost any career. Be it conventional litigation, business, teaching, or military, a firm foundation in legal analysis and knowledge can lend itself greatly to your success."
 –Lawyer–Product Liability Law, Boca Raton, FL

"I needed a challenge—I wanted to have a strong legal foundation for my entrepreneurial work."
 –Law Student, San Francisco, CA

"I wanted a practical foundation for the rest of my career. And it was a good fit for me because I love logic, argument, and persuasion."
 –Law Student, Dallas, TX

"*I believed that knowledge of the law, which is the foundation of our society and affects everyone's life at one point or another, was a powerful tool and whether I decided to practice or not it would be invaluable.*"

**–Lawyer–Mergers and Acquisitions,
San Antonio, TX**

To Make a Difference

"*I decided to go to law school in 2003, at a time when current and world events became increasingly intertwined with interesting legal issues. It really made me think about the difference I could make with a law degree. As I started to think about all the possibilities, it became clear that I should go to law school.*"

–Lawyer–Criminal Law, Chicago, IL

"I had been working with multiple attorneys through a victim's assistance program and noticed that some victims did not get the representation they deserved from their attorneys, and therefore they became a victim for a second time. It was at that point, I decided to go to law school and challenge myself to do my best to help those in need of representation at the most important times in their life."

–Law Student, Boston, MA

"I had recently attended a swearing in ceremony for the SJPD and had been contemplating a graduate degree (most likely an MBA) at the time of the ceremony. The speech given by the chief of police inspired me to go to law school so that I could enter a profession where I could make a difference and perhaps be remembered for the difference that I made."

–Student, Mishawaka, IN

" *After being in the 'real world' for a few years, I knew that I wanted to make a difference in the world, and that law school would most likely be the way for me to do that.* "

–Lawyer–Mergers and Acquisitions, Pembroke Pines, FL

" *I finally decided to listen to my conscience. I was working in sales and doing quite well, but something was missing. I felt like I had talent and ability that could be used to make a real difference in people's lives by practicing law. Law school and my subsequent summer work has confirmed that I made the right choice.* "

–Lawyer–Intellectual Property Law, Columbus, OH

"Some friends of mine were arrested and put through the system after [political] protests . . . After seeing what happened to them while they were in custody, just getting brutalized physically and psychologically, I developed an interest in the law and eventually ended up applying to law school."

–Law Student, Washington, DC

"I wanted to get the kind of education that would allow me to help shape my community."

–Law Student, Philadelphia, PA

Career Change

"I am a career-changer. My previous one wasn't fulfilling, and I needed to do something different."

–Lawyer–Environmental Law, Syracuse, NY

"*I had reached a point in my career where I was making decent money but it just wasn't making me happy. I wanted to do something more substantial with my life. So after getting at least a little more financially set (recovering from old undergraduate debt), I decided that I had put off law school for far too long. It's been totally worth it.*"

—Law Student, San Francisco, CA

"*At the time I was a modern dancer in New York City, with myriad jobs (including yoga teacher, dance teacher, personal assistant, waitress, legal proofreader, etc.). I wanted to have just one job and have it be something that made me proud. So I chose public interest law.*"

—Law Student, Cincinnati, OH

The Fact of the Matter

Overall employment of new law graduates has been close to or above 89 percent since 1997, with significant increases seen in 2005 and 2006. The employment rate for the law school class of 2006 was 90.7 percent—it was the highest it has been since 2000.

(Source: National Association of Legal Professionals, Bulletin, July 2007)

"After working full time for four years in advertising, I realized I was more interested in analyzing the contracts than the ads. I never even considered law school until a colleague stated the obvious—you should be a lawyer, not an advertiser!"

–Lawyer–Employment Law, San Antonio, TX

The Fact of the Matter

In a 2006 study on "second career" lawyers, the National Association of Legal Placement found that "second-career lawyers reported a wide variety of prior careers, including accounting, banking/finance, journalism/writing, human resources, insurance, marketing/public relations, real estate, retail sales, and management. Less commonly reported backgrounds were biomedical research, food service manager, art director/illustrator, landscape architect, pharmaceutical scientist, chemistry research and development, theological seminary admissions and distance education, puppeteer, union field representative, and refugee relief."

(Source: National Association of Legal Professionals, NALP Research on Second Career Lawyers, 2004)

"At the age of 33, I felt like there was no time better than the present. I didn't want to look back during my old age and wonder if I could have done it."

—Lawyer–Business Law, Teaneck, NJ

"*I came to the realization that in three years I'd be three years older regardless of whether or not I went to law school. Made the decision to do it in my mid-30s much easier.*"
   –Law Student, New York, NY

"*It was the right thing to do. I was a non-traditional student. I took almost 10 years between high school and undergrad and then I had been working in banking for five years. Law is always where I wanted to be and I saw no reason why just because I was a little older than most students I couldn't do it.*"
   –Law Student, Portland, OR

"When I turned 30 I looked around me and wondered how in the world I ended up as an analyst in retail. By the time I decided to go to law school I was worried, because by the time I would graduate I would be 36. But I decided I'd rather be 36 and a lawyer than 36 and still in retail. Have not regretted my decision even once."

—Lawyer–Bankruptcy Law, Miami, FL

The Fact of the Matter

A recent study of law students found that approximately two-thirds enrolled either directly (37 percent) or one to two years (30 percent) following their undergrad. Eighteen percent, however, enrolled three to five years after finishing college and 9 percent stated that it had been six to ten years. Fully 7 percent of respondents entered law school more than 10 years after earning an undergraduate degree.

(Source: LSSSE 2006 Annual Survey Results, Engaging Legal Education: Moving Beyond the Status Quo, Law School Survey of Student Engagement, Indiana University Center for Postsecondary Research, www.lssse.iub.edu)

" *I was coming out of a writing career that offered very solitary challenges, and I was interested in working in a team-oriented environment. I knew the law would offer a nice combination of independence and group challenges.* "
–Law Student, Philadelphia, PA

THE ACADEMIC CHALLENGE

Make no mistake—most will find law school to be academically challenging. The workload can be demanding and the competition fierce. Most also find it intellectually stimulating and incredibly rewarding.

" *Attending law school was not always a dream, but a desire. I enjoyed the courtroom and trial work. The horrible stories of law school really motivated me. I was up for the challenge.* "
–Lawyer–Medical Malpractice, Sacramento, CA

" *I wanted the academic and intellectual challenge and I was tired of working in politics.* "
   –Law Student, New York, NY

" *I realized I was way too smart for my job and needed to move on with my life in a way that would challenge me.* "
   –Law Student, San Diego, CA

" *The faculty was the most important factor when deciding to go to law school. Also, I strongly considered the students, and general atmosphere of the school.* "
   –Lawyer–Intellectual Property Law, Beverly Hills, CA

" *During my senior year of college, one of my professors gave me the following advice: 'If there is any ounce left in you that can handle any more school, then you should do it.' I chose to go to law school right after I finished college because it was just the right time for me.* "

–Lawyer–Product Liability Law, New York, NY

" *I chose law school because I knew it would open up a world of job opportunities where I could use and exercise my brain every day. Fortunately I found a job in my last year of law school where I can do just that. I was challenged as a law student in the job and when I return in the fall after taking the bar exam, I'll continue to be challenged.* "

–Law Student, Minneapolis, MN

Inside Tip

If you have always wanted to be a lawyer, but you are not exactly sure what area of law interests you, don't worry! In fact, it is probably best to go into law school keeping an open mind about what area you are interested in—once you know more about the legal system, you will be pulled toward a field.

MONEY, MONEY, MONEY

Despite what many think, law school is not a first-class ticket to easy street. Can lawyers make incredible salaries their first year out of school? Yes. At the same time, not everyone who attends law school will want this type of reward. Law school is a significant investment of both time and money, and the return you'll get is related to the investment you'll put in. After all, law is a profession—almost everyone involved is there to make a living practicing it!

"*Working in the court system, I was tired of doing the attorney's jobs for them. So I decided to go, so that I could make the money for the work I was doing anyway.*"
–Law Student, Miami, FL

"*I wanted to work for myself, have flexible hours, and still make great money. All with the chance to make a difference in people's lives.*"
–Lawyer–Employment Law, Montrose, PA

The Fact of the Matter

According to the 2006 *Associate Salary Survey* from the National Association of Legal Career Professionals, the median first-year associate salary for firms with more than 500 attorneys rose to $135,000 in 2006. The median starting salary for all firms, regardless of size, was $105,000.

(Source: National Association of Legal Career Professionals, 2006 Associate Salary Survey)

> *"As an accountant, I was tired of counting other people's money and working to make money for someone other than me."*
> **—Lawyer–Mergers and Acquisitions, Hallandale Beach, FL**

There are multiple reasons people choose to enter the legal profession. For some it will be in pursuit of their first career while for others it will be to change their current line of work. Others may plan to do something different with their JD and not choose to practice law at all. Recognize that whatever your reason for wanting to go to law school there are some real challenges—but also some real rewards—ahead of you. With the right mindset, and a good idea of what to expect, the path to your JD is not something you should be afraid of!

CHAPTER 2

Law School Myths Debunked

"Don't believe all the horror stories about the teachers and amount of work. If you keep up on your reading and pay attention in class, the rest will fall into place. Law school is not easy by any means, but it can be enjoyable if you have the right attitude."

–Law Student, New York, NY

Rumors abound regarding what it is like to attend law school, many of them fueled by movies that portray it as a dog-eat-dog world where only a few survive. The reality is that almost all students make it through and many (or most) even look back fondly at their years in school. Sure, law school can sometimes be a grind—you didn't think it was going to be a three-year party did you? But it can also be a great experience—one where you will meet a lot of people with a similar mindset who are all facing a common challenge.

MYTH: 1L IS HELL

> *"I've never learned more in my life than during 1L. I look at the world in a new way. It was worth every second."*
>
> **–Law Student, Phoenix, AZ**

" *Your 1L year is the defining year. Make the
most of it!* "

–Lawyer–Legal Malpractice Law, Rochester, NY

" *Of course, law school is tough, but it isn't
absolute hell. It's more like that pesky
paper cut you accidentally spill vinegar on
... it stings a little from time to time, but
in the end it's only superficial. If you just
focus on learning and take an active role
in your own emergence into the
profession, you'll hardly notice it.* "

–Law Student, Los Angeles, CA

MYTH: LAW SCHOOL IS ALL WORK AND NO PLAY

There is a significant amount of stress
inherent in trying to learn to "think like a
lawyer," and you will find yourself wanting to
blow off some of that steam. And, of course,

your classmates are going through the exact same experience. In addition to enjoying the intellectual stimulation, law school is also full of social events and clubs.

> *" You don't have to check your social life at your undergrad graduation. You can still enjoy a healthy social life and do very well. Law school just teaches you time allocation—the exact skill you will need the rest of your life."*
> —**Law Student, Cambridge, MA**

> *" Emotionally and socially it's like a mix between lunch during middle school and Friday nights in undergrad."*
> —**Lawyer–Legal Malpractice Law, Clinton Township, MI**

"*The relationships you form not only keep you sane but create a great network base for the future. After all, unless you move out of your law school's state after school, you are going to be working with your classmates well after you graduate.*"

–Lawyer–Mergers and Acquisitions, New York, NY

Inside Tip

Law schools typically have an active social scene as students look to blow off steam from the challenges of the day. While these are great activities to participate in, make sure you do them in moderation!

"*The most interesting myth about law school is that it is a terrible experience. I totally disagree. Law school has been a hundred times more interesting and rewarding than undergrad.*"

–Law Student, Portland, OR

> "You can do very well and still have fun, and in fact I did some of my best work when I was not stressed out. Don't give up who you are and what you love just because you are in law school."
>
> **–Lawyer–Elder Law, Fresno, CA**

> "Being in the night program at my school made me appreciate my time and get more out of it as opposed to the day students. At first I was intimidated when they signed up for some of my classes because I thought that they would have more time to study, but in actuality I made better use of my 'less' time."
>
> **–Law Student, Detroit, MI**

MYTH: HALF THE CLASS WILL FAIL

Thirty years ago, rumor had it that some first-year professors would say on the first day—"Look to your left, look to your right, look at yourself; one of you won't be here next year." While this may have once had an element of truth, it is no longer the case. Most students make it through, and those that do not typically leave for personal reasons.

"It's a myth that lots of people will flunk out. The whole 'look to your left, look to your right, and one of these people will not make it through to be hooded' was a complete farce. Anyone who didn't make it through to graduation was a drop out, not a flunk out. Which means that it is stupid to drop out for fear of flunking out because it is most likely not going to happen in the absence of some flagrant error on your part."

–Lawyer–Environmental Law, Wyandotte, MI

The Fact of the Matter
The attrition rate of law students during four years of law school is less than 5 percent for all ABA approved law schools. Many schools—particularly top schools—actually have significantly *lower* rates of attrition. For example, the top 10 law schools (based on average LSAT score of the 1L class) have a four-year attrition rate of less than 1 percent.

(Source: Official Guide to ABA Approved Law Schools, LSAC and ABA, 2007)

"As long as you can read, you can get through the material—but you'd better make the time commitment."

–Lawyer–Mergers and Acquisitions, Portland, OR

"A constantly heard myth is that undergrad is significantly easier than law school, simply because of the number of chances one has to improve. In law school you get one exam—that's it. Make the most of it by studying diligently, and by doing old exams."

–Law Student, Houston, TX

"Law school is not impossible and if you put the hard work into it, you will succeed and be just fine."

–Law Student, San Francisco, CA

"Biggest myths: Success before law school dictates success in law school, and that the smarter the person, the better they do in law school. Biggest truth: There is absolutely no substitute for hard work, but more than that, consistent work is crucial."

–Lawyer–Trusts and Estates, Eastpointe, MI

"Comparing undergrad to law school is like comparing apples to oranges. The skill sets it takes to succeed are different enough, that success in one does not necessarily rely on being successful in the other. I was a C student in college and an A student in law school. Go figure."

–Lawyer–Litigation, Jackson, MS

"The myth is that everyone is smarter than you. I went into law school coming from a state university and was completely intimidated by my classmates from Harvard, Yale, etc. However, starting out with this presumption was only setting myself up for failure. After seeing my Harvard classmates squirm in their seats when called on, and even get a few questions wrong, I started to realize we are all in the same boat—granted, some people will try to push you out of the boat."

–Law Student, Los Angeles, CA

MYTH: IT'S ABOUT LEARNING THE LAW

You go to law school to learn the law, right? Well, not exactly. In truth, you go to law school to learn how to think and analyze like a lawyer. Part of what will make first year so confounding will be professors' attempts to hide the "law" from you. Don't get discouraged—this is the learning process that everyone goes through.

"Here is the most interesting quote I remember (from a professor no less): 'You learn a lot of things in law school, but law is not one of them.'"

–Lawyer–Class Action Law, Houston, TX

"There was a big gap between the classroom lectures and the material that actually needed to be learned for success on the exams. It was not until my second year that I realized law school was not really meant to teach you the law, but more how to think and analyze. Learning the law was something that you did on your own, and that was what you were tested on."

–Law Student, Palo Alto, CA

"I heard a lot about the reading in law school and I imagined that classes would involve memorizing huge books of 'law.' This is not what law school is! In undergrad you can always go to class whether you read or not—in law school you can't. You must read and look up all the words that you don't understand BEFORE class. You must be prepared to recite and to 'think like a lawyer.'"

–Lawyer–Trusts and Estates, Chicago, IL

" *A major myth is that all you need to study is to read the course books like you did while in undergrad. The truth is study guides are heaven-sent!* "

–Law Student, San Diego, CA

" *Build up your reading stamina for law school; you will need it. You have a lot less free time in law school so use it wisely.* "

–Law Student, Chicago, IL

" *I didn't realize just how taxing law school would be. Three hours of studying in undergrad is nothing like three hours of studying in law school. It takes way more energy out of you.* "

–Lawyer–Civil Rights Law, Eagan, MN

❝Don't go to law school unless you really, really want it. It's not like three more years of slightly hard undergrad.❞
–Law Student, Denver, CO

❝I miss the way that performance in undergrad classes actually correlated to how hard I worked and prepared. My performance in law school classes appeared to have most to do with format of the exam (in class, take home, or paper), and how well I understood the teacher (I always did better in class with a teacher with a similar way of approaching problems).❞
–Lawyer–Intellectual Property Law, Lafayette, CA

❝Law school teaches you how to think and analyze in a certain way.❞
–Law Student, San Francisco, CA

" *The first year is the hardest year because you are not learning for content but to change the way you think. It is a myth that the second and third year become easier—in fact you just learn how to processes the material quicker.* "

–Lawyer–Real Estate Law, Jackson, MI

" *I really was not aware of many truths or myths prior to law school. I came from a blue-collar family and entered law school blind to the experience I was about to undertake. However, I quickly realized that the Socratic method is just as brutal as it is portrayed in the movies.* "

–Lawyer–Civil Rights Law, Chicago, IL

" *Not only does law school demand more work, it demands much more analytical thinking. Memorization is not the key to law school exams; law school takes learning several steps further.* "

–Law Student, Denver, CO

> **"** *Essentially I vacationed through undergrad, so I had a lot of catching up to do on learning how to study when I got to law school, but I still don't think it was as hard as everyone said it would be.* **"**
> **–Lawyer–Trial Law, Saint Paul, MN**

MYTH: THE CUTTHROAT COMPETITION WILL EAT YOU ALIVE

You know that law is a competitive discipline and assume that law school must be a harrowing experience. The reality is that at most law schools, this is not the case. Sure students are competitive, and sometimes this can go over the top. But for the most part, it is a friendly competition. Make friends early and learn which students to trust as part of your circle of friends—these relationships will be a great resource both in school and once you graduate.

A great benefit of spending three years with the same group of people is that they will become your extended professional network after law school. Moreover, the relationships you form in your law school career will be invaluable. The very people that you competed with for grades in school, you will call upon to help you solve a particularly tough legal issue once you are practicing. As most attorneys specialize once they leave school, you will find that you can draw upon a wealth of expertise just from your class. Law school is the time to develop the type of relationships that allow you to pick up the phone and pose a question or ask a favor a few years down the road.

Your classmates will start to share outlines and study notes just as quickly as you do. Remember to keep perspective. The competitiveness can drive you but should not numb you. There will always be someone that it seems is in the library more, has more outlines, or is just studying more than you are. You have to pace yourself against your own threshold and your own learning style. You will want to know how much time you can devote to your reading and your studying and stick with your plan. Don't change your course just because someone else appears to be doing more!

Inside Tip

If you are a very competitive individual, then there are great opportunities for you. Work to join law review. Join moot court. Participate in the various competitions that your law school has to offer. They are great for expanding your thinking and your skills and play very well to highly competitive people.

"Do not let what other students tell you affect your studying. Everyone is different and those who tell you they have already outlined the class after week three or that they study until midnight seven days a week are lying."

–Law Student, Raleigh, NC

"*Law school is not necessarily more difficult than undergrad. It is only the stress put on students by other students that makes it seem so.*"

–Law Student, Dallas, TX

"*Do not worry about what other 1Ls are doing, and especially ignore what some 1Ls claim they do. Some students try to psych other students out by claiming to study 20 hours a day. They are either lying, or they will become so burned out by the time finals start that they will not perform well on exams.*"

–Lawyer–Intellectual Property Law, Bowie, MD

"*Don't be arrogant or pretentious as you are surrounded by people with high intellectual rigor who will take note.*"

–Law Student, Washington, DC

"It is true that law students can be incredibly selfish and petty, and I think that's the worst thing about law school—you really do learn your fellow students' true nature in such a stressful and demanding experience. However, you also find those people who are more laid back and easy to get along with (although they are few and far between), and those people redeem the experience."

–Lawyer–Legal Malpractice Law, North Liberty, IA

"Don't listen to rumors spread by nervous students!"

–Lawyer–Mergers and Acquisitions, New York, NY

"*I always heard about how competitive law school is. To the extent that you are graded on a curve against your classmates, this is true. But I never saw anyone act in an underhanded way. For the most part, people are happy to share outlines, answer questions, and help out if they can.*"

–Law Student, New York, NY

"*It is as competitive as they say, but people are more friendly than they let on.*"

–Lawyer–Real Estate Law, Cary, NC

"*Law school is competitive if you allow it to be. Generally you can do your own thing and you do not have to get caught up in that.*"

–Law Student, Philadelphia, PA

" *Law school is highly competitive and most of the students there are type A, highly motivated, and ambitious people.* "
–Law Student, Milwaukee, WI

" *Students at my law school were not as competitive with other students. No one was stealing cases or ripping pages out of books. Students competed mostly with themselves to do their best possible.* "
–Lawyer–Litigation, Albany, NY

" *Law school is not a joke. People come into it thinking that it's going to be similar to undergrad. You will be surrounded by many different types of students including returning students who have been working or raising families full-time. It is very hard for some students to adjust to not partying seven days a week.* "
–Law Student, New York, NY

"Students with your approximate same age and experience who are in your year are invaluable toward helping you survive. It's hard to be a "nontraditional" student among a class of people who have never really had a job or had to live on their own."

–Law Student, Boston, MA

"It is highly competitive, and when you are a 1L, every little event or drama has the potential to knock you out of orbit. If I could go back, I would try to avoid all the comparisons and rumors and panic talk. Taking it in stride and not focusing on those nuisances would have made it much more peaceful during my first year."

–Lawyer–Bankruptcy Law, Columbia, SC

"Because of the forced curve for the required courses, students get very competitive. These are the same people you'll be with for three or four years. So you may meet your worst enemy, and/or you may meet friends that you'll remain close to."

–Lawyer–Real Estate Law, Boston, MA

"A myth is that people are out to get you (e.g., hiding books, falsifying notes). I guess it depends on the school but mine fostered a supportive—rather than competitive—environment. Of course, people are competitive with grades and in class but no one was out to get others—notes and outlines were shared and it was a very collegial atmosphere."

–Law Student, Providence, RI

"*Spend time with your colleagues and become friends with them. The relationships that you fomr here will be more valuable 20 years from now than your GPA.*"

–Law Student, Los Angeles, CA

"*Make sure to talk to other students who had your professors previously so you know what to expect in the classroom and for the final.*"

–Lawyer–Business Law, Jenkintown, PA

Inside Tip

Take time to surround yourself with those that have similar study skills as you start law school. As you get into the groove, start to seek out opportunities to spend time with those who have a different style or who approach their thinking differently. It will broaden your thinking in invaluable ways.

"*Make friends with your classmates and peers and then be a mentor to underclassmates. One day you will need them and they will need you. It's a networking field.*"
–Lawyer–Class Action Law, Brooklyn, NY

"*Study groups are great but you should be selective who you study with; they can adversely affect you. However once that group is determined, those friends will be with you for a lifetime after graduation. Do not believe gossip or rumors in law school dealing with grades or classmates. Your experiences with classmates will determine whether you would want to have them represent you in the future once they pass the bar exam or as a friend and study partner.*"
–Law Student, Chicago, IL

"*It is a myth that law school is cutthroat and competitive (I found it competitive, but also quite cooperative). Professors are Socratic and scary and will humiliate you (they are certainly Socratic, especially 1L year) but if you adjust to it and take it for what it's worth, you can see the benefit of that teaching style.*"

–Law Student, Los Angeles, CA

"*Everyone in law school is ultracompetitive but not to the point of being dishonest and doing things such as hiding books in the library. Most people in my experience also have enough class that they would not go out of their way to put other students at a disadvantage. Most people want to do well by preparing and learning the material, and getting the best score on the exam. You are going to be with these people for three years and a sense of camaraderie can help you stay sane, especially come exam time.*"

–Lawyer–Bankruptcy Law, Seminole, FL

"*Breathe. You are all in this together. It will all work out. Take it in small, manageable steps while knowing each step will bring you one step closer to becoming a lawyer. Remember it is the journey and not the destination that is important.*"

–Lawyer–Intellectual Property Law, LaGrange, GA

"*The biggest myth in law school is the fact that you can't be friends with your classmates because they are out to get you. Law school taught me not just how to study the law but also how to deal with people! Be a civil person and people will reciprocate with civility.*"

–Lawyer–Elder Law, Fair Oaks, CA

" *Absolutely don't allow yourself to get caught up in the competition with other students. There is absolutely NOTHING to be gained from it, except for enemies. It is true what they tell you, that once you graduate everyone in your class is going to be your colleagues, and there is something to be said for having built good relation-ships while you are in school.* "

–Law Student, Baltimore, MD

" *The emphasis many people place on the competitiveness of law school has been, in my experience, unfounded. It may be the case at some schools but it isn't always and doesn't have to be the case at any school.* "

–Law Student, Miami, FL

MYTH: BEING A PRE-LAW MAJOR WILL MAKE LAW SCHOOL EASIER

Law school assumes you arrive on day one with little or no understanding of the law. Whether this is true or not in your particular case, you probably do not understand it the way they want you to. Save the study of law until you get to law school—you'll have plenty of opportunity to do it once you're there!

> " It's a myth that if you had a legal job prior to law school, this will give you an advantage over other students. "
> —Law Student, Dallas, TX

> " You are just as smart and capable of doing well in law school as others who are older, wiser, have more work experience, or have more academic degrees than you do. "
> —Law Student, New York, NY

MYTH: YOU WILL DROWN IN TUITION AND FEES

Many students attending law school will have to find some way of paying for school on their own or through scholarships. Of course, if you are living on loans, you should work hard to minimize expenses during your three years at school. An old saying goes "if you live like a lawyer while you are in law school, you will live like a law student while you are lawyer." To help you with this, there are a number of organizations that can help you manage the process of taking loans and paying for your education. Many of these will be handled before your first year, but you also may apply for some scholarships while you are in school.

> "*I had a good GPA and a good LSAT score, so my law school offered me a 60 percent scholarship. That equated to about $18,000 per year, which is an amount that I could not refuse.*"
> **—Lawyer–Elder Law, Washington, DC**

> **The Fact of the Matter**
> Over 13 percent of full-time law students receive financial aid scholarships of between 50 and 100 percent of their tuition.

(Source: Official Guide to ABA Approved Law Schools, LSAC and ABA, 2007)

" I know the pressure to get into firms is very high, but if that is not what you are interested in, seek what your heart desires; there are many scholarships, and other forms of financial support for public interest or international internships."

–Lawyer–Civil Rights Law, Gilbert, AZ

There are many myths regarding the first year of law school. Whether in the movies or books or through friends who have "been through it and lived to tell," there never seems to be a shortage of horror stories about how bad it will be. The reality is that law school, while far from easy, is much more manageable than these stories would lead you to believe. Law school will involve a significant amount of work and the "new" approach to learning can be a bit of a shock. It is not, however, going to be the nightmare you may imagine. In fact, the shared experience of going through school will probably lead to some great memories and friendships. Hopefully, the Voices of Experience have convinced you not to let these myths prevent you from pursuing your dream of being an attorney.

CHAPTER 3

Starting Off on the Right Foot

"I thought that law school was going to be like undergrad with more reading. I was so wrong. Law school was unlike anything I had ever done before."

—Lawyer—Business Law, New York, NY

The first day is going to feel like you are starting something really big—and you are! It is going to be the first day of the next three years and it is going to start with a bang. Unlike in undergrad, classes start at full speed on day one. Remember—everyone in your first-year class got good grades in college, had a good LSAT score, and really wants to finish law school—you'll have to work hard just to be above average.

> *The bottom line is that if you don't want to study the law, if you truly have no passion for it whatsoever, then law school will be torture, you will hate all three years and you are better off spending $100,000 elsewhere. But, if you do enjoy the law and in your heart aspire to be an attorney, then you will find the path for success much easier than undergrad because everything you learn will be an open door of interest.*
> —Law Student, Memphis, TN

IT'S NOT UNDERGRAD

The first year is going to involve absorbing a lot of information while learning (or, for some, refining) a way of thinking about issues. For most students, the experience will be totally different from what they saw in undergrad. Recognizing that things will require a new level of discipline is half the challenge; approach law school prepared to put in the needed effort and you will do fine.

"The main thing: Don't take everything so seriously, and don't get psyched out by peer pressure. The curve isn't as bad as people make it out to be. Do your very best to keep up—if you consistently read your assignments, you'll never feel slammed, and you'll be pretty well prepared when it's time for exams. If you fall behind on your reading, that's when you'll feel overwhelmed. Make time for sleep, exercise, a social life, and some pro bono. People make a big deal about the 1L year, but your LIFE will be busy if you're going to be a lawyer, and you need to learn how to make room for priorities starting now."

–Lawyer–Environmental Law, Weston, FL

"Law school is a different animal than undergrad. Law school is more intense and it is easier to fall behind if you don't stay on top of the reading assignments."

–Law Student, Houston, TX

"I thought I was coming to law school to learn, but instead I was told that I was there to become."

–Law Student, Boston, MA

"I learned more and studied more in my first semester of law school than I did in my entire bachelor's and master's programs (and I went to great schools!)."

–Lawyer–Criminal Law, San Francisco, CA

"I thought undergrad was challenging; law school was a wake-up call. It was difficult, but it's a lot more satisfying when you finish."

–Lawyer–Trial Law, Brandon, MS

"*Just like college, it will take you a semester or so to really figure out how much studying and preparing you need to do for each class. But the bottom line is you will need to do much more than undergrad to stay ahead of the game.*"
   –Law Student, Sacramento, CA

"*I was surprised how few people acted any differently than an undergrad right out of high school. It showed on exam day when those who treated law school like a job got As and Bs while those who treated it like 'Undergrad: Part Two' got Cs and Ds.*"
   –Lawyer–Product Liability Law, Maryville, IL

"*It is true that it is a lot more work [than college]. Reading assignments are 10 times the length they were in undergrad. In law school, everyone you see will be just as smart as you.*"
   –Lawyer–Mergers and Acquisitions, Palisade, CO

"I began law school assuming that I would be tested at the same level of generality as in college. But I now appreciate that the expertise demanded of a lawyer is on a par with the skill level one would expect of a surgeon. It gets easier, but in the meantime try to keep a steady hand."

–Lawyer–Product Liability Law, Little River, TX

"Remember, study smart AND hard. Only 0.01 percent can slack off, not go to class, and still do well. You MUST go to class."

–Law Student, Philadelphia, PA

"Undergrad courses teach from the broad concept and work in, while law courses work from narrow concepts and work out. It took two years for me to realize that."

–Lawyer–Bankruptcy Law, New York, NY

*" You cannot just 'get by' in law school . . .
you must read and study to understand."*
–Lawyer–Class Action Law, Hoboken, NJ

*" It is important to realize that law school is
a totally different world. I received my
undergraduate degree in pre-law, and this
was still totally different than anything I'd
ever done before. The sooner one realizes
that you don't know anything about law
school or the law as you must know it for
law school, the sooner you can adjust your
mind to begin to enter and conquer this
new world. (Besides, no one else there will
know anything yet, either.)"*
–Law Student, San Antonio, TX

BEFORE THE FIRST DAY

Almost all ABA approved law schools will
teach the same subjects during the first year.

And almost all of these 1L classes will have a reading assignment for the first class. It also helps to be prepared for the first day in other ways (many schools will have a summer reading list). In law school, the first session of a class is a day like any other—you can expect the professor to jump right in and begin calling on students by name. Like on every other day—be prepared!

> *"Read books about the law school experience the summer beforehand. Learn how to brief cases—facts, issue, rule, analysis, reasoning, holding, dicta, dissent—and see whether certain methods, such as color-coding, help you recall and find the material when called upon in class."*
>
> **–Lawyer–Mergers and Acquisitions, Alexandria, VA**

"Visit your law school before you decide to enroll there. Ask them for a tour of the facilities, and if possible, sit in on a class to see what it is like. I did."

–Law Student, New York, NY

"Read MANY 'how to succeed in law school' books to learn the ropes. Everything you feel and experience during your first year is fully explained in those books. When you feel like the 'dumbest person in the room,' or when you get grilled by a professor, or when you finally understand a difficult topic, you will be motivated if you've read that others before you have gone through the same and survived."

–Lawyer–Employment Law, Marietta, GA

"Find out everything you can about law school before you go to law school—from the classes, the structure, the homework, the expectations, the profs—everything. Then make sure you're ready for it— that you're ready to commit and make it a priority."

–Lawyer–Trial Law, Orlando, FL

"If you don't know anything about the law or law school, try to take some kind of an introductory course over the summer so that you can learn basic skills like IRAC."

–Law Student, San Francisco, CA

"I think that students should start studying for law school at least three weeks before law school actually starts. I recommend listening to course CDs and taking notes (typing can be a great way to take them) in order to obtain a general background related to the course material."

–Law Student, New York, NY

YOU CANNOT HIDE, SO BE PREPARED

For most law students, law school will be your introduction to a teaching style known as the Socratic method—teaching through question and answer. Your professor—a "black belt" in the art of the Socratic method—will force you to examine all aspects of legal cases by interrogating you on your understanding of the material. The professor will frequently call on students at random from a seating chart he or she has prepared (you usually choose your seat the first day). Your best defense? Be prepared because it could be you.

" *Be prepared for class; you will get called on!* "
   –Lawyer–Business Law, Healdsburg, CA

" *Always be prepared for class, and be persistent with your studying.* "
   –Law Student, St. Louis, MO

The Fact of the Matter
A recent study of law students found that 51 percent of students discovered they worked harder than they ever thought they could to meet faculty members' standards or expectations. The study also found that 83 percent of students came to class with readings or assignments completed.

(Source: LSSSE 2006 Annual Survey Results Overview, Engaging Legal Education: Moving Beyond the Status Quo, Law School Survey of Student Engagement, Indiana University Center for Postsecondary Research, www.lssse.iub.edu)

"*Have good organizational skills, and always be prepared. The experience is not as tough when looking back on things, so don't be frustrated or agitated by the experience, the material is not that difficult and you will succeed if you put in the work.*"

–Lawyer–Mergers and Acquisitions, Falls Church, VA

" *Be organized and prepared for class. Make sure you understand something before you move on. And ask questions!* "
   –Law Student, San Francisco, CA

" *Be organized, be prepared, and realize that a lot of it is just a mind game. They're trying to figure out who should make the cut.* "
   –Law Student, Boston, MA

" *Study, study, study! There's no such thing as too much preparation. Read the cases even though they might be boring and confusing.* "
   –Lawyer–Class Action Law, Washington, DC

" *Be as prepared as you can all the time. Do all of your assignments diligently and as far in advance as you can. Try not to get caught up in the competition, but be extremely competitive with yourself.* "
   –Law Student, Los Angeles, CA

> *"I was not prepared for the amount of work expected of us. In addition to strategies for doing well on exams, it would have been helpful to have been given a sense of just how much time and effort first year would be."*
>
> **–Lawyer–Litigationm, Oakland, CA**

SET EXPECTATIONS EARLY

While law school is not going to be the end of your social life, it will be an enormous time commitment. Many family members and significant others can have a hard time adjusting to the reality of your life as a law student. Set expectations early and remember—it does get more manageable after the first year.

> *"Appreciate the dedication required in terms of both your personal time and your relationships."*
>
> **–Law Student, Los Angeles, CA**

"*Don't be overwhelmed. Just take it one day at a time and really focus on why you decided to go to law school and don't get distracted by friends and family pulling you away from your study. Don't get me wrong, you need a break every now and again, but don't let that become an everyday or weekend occurrence.*"

–Law Student, Dallas, TX

"*If your friends and family have not been through law school themselves, they will not understand what it takes to be in your position—while you will find the occasional law student who is more interested in partying and socializing, 90 percent of the students are there to study.*"

–Lawyer–Business Law, San Francisco, CA

"*If you are married or in a relationship, do not assume that your significant other really understands (or can ever understand) what you are going through. Do not complain to them. Do not discuss legal issues with them and expect them to understand. Don't let law school impact your relationship; law school is temporary—they are not. Brace yourself, it will be a wild (and ultimately worthwhile) endeavor.*"

–Law Student, Miami, FL

"*Do your best to maintain balance between the law and your personal life while maintaining your time effectively. This may seem to be quite impossible, but, in retrospect, I think that you will find that it was quite necessary.*"

–Lawyer–Mergers and Acquisitions, Hyattsville, MD

MANAGE STRESS, DON'T LET IT MANAGE YOU

Of course law school will sometimes be stressful—it is a lot of work on an important subject where you are trying to do your best! The important thing is to make sure that the stress does not become overwhelming. Take time out to do things outside of law school that are important to you and that allow you to "decompress." You will return to your studies with a clearer head and better able to manage the volume of work required.

"I was a deer in headlights for much of my first year of law school. I was absolutely terrified of the Socratic method, and spent many first-year classes in silent prayer to not be called on, even though I had manically outlined and read each case. I was so intimidated that a teacher could have called on me and asked me my home address, and I wouldn't have known it. Looking back, it was silly. I should have had more confidence in myself and been more aware of everyone else feeling the same way. If you read, outline, and simply do the work that is asked of you, you can conquer anything a professor may ask you when called on. I was so afraid to say 'I don't know,' when in reality there were so many things none of us knew or could have been expected to know, but you're there to be challenged so you need to expect those kinds of questions."

–Lawyer–Civil Rights Law, Brooklyn, NY

"*Do not stress out! Stress and idle chitchat about how 'hard' law school is, is a waste of time and energy better spent actually studying for class or spending much-needed quality time with family and friends. Law school should not define you, it should refine you. Stay who you are, just become a better version of you.*"

–Lawyer–Intellectual Property Law, Tempe, AZ

"*Don't panic. It's like nothing you've ever experienced before. Figure out what will work best for you and discard all advice to contrary—doing something that works for others may not be the best strategy for you.*"

–Law Student, San Diego, CA

" *You don't have to kill yourself; be sure to make time for yourself as well as friends and family. You need to have balance in order to make it through.* "

—**Law Student, San Diego, CA**

" *Don't be scared. Your grades and your academic standing and your under-standing of the material doesn't come as easy as it did for most students in under-graduate. But that's the point . . . you have to learn to fight through that and not let things like that stop you from being a good student, a good advocate, and a good lawyer!! Everything is possible . . . nothing is impossible . . . just look at everyone who has done it before you. Just don't forget to take the time to take a breath every now and then. Everyone needs to!* "

—**Law Student, Washington, DC**

"*Don't let the stress of those around you get you down. I fainted my first year, three weeks before exams. As I fell to the ground, my head hit the counter. I knocked myself out in addition to fainting. It was on my way out of the law school on a gurney that I wondered if I had made a mistake. Three years later I walked across the stage with a diploma in my hands. It takes hard work and perseverance. If you can make it through the first semester, you can make it through to the end.*"

–Lawyer–Criminal Law, Little Rock, AR

Inside Tip

Try to find what works best in terms of studying schedule and location early on. For example, if you live in a noisy environment, it may be best to visit the law library after classes to prepare for the next day.

"*Don't get overwhelmed. Organize your study time and still read the cases even if you don't understand them ... always be prepared because even if you try the professor will teach in such a method that you should grasp the material. Remember, if others can do it, you can too.*"

–Law Student, Philadelphia, PA

"*Don't stress out just because you think everyone around you is understanding the material and you aren't. Remember, your classmates all have different life experiences; they might have come into the class with some understanding of the law beforehand. It will click for you in time, but you've got to put the work in.*"

–Law Student, Baltimore, MD

"*I was out of undergrad for 10 years before going to law school, and the intensity (and craziness) of some of the people coming right out of college was annoying. Not that you shouldn't be intense, but don't be crazy. People that worked before going to law school were far more normal and palatable than the kids.*"

–Lawyer–Bankruptcy Law, Columbus, OH

"*I was told that it was okay as an undergrad to be a 'lazy genius' but that it wouldn't work in law school. Except I was and I still graduated at the top of my class. It's all about studying in a way that is conducive to you learning the law and understanding its implications, not about how many hours you spend studying.*"

–Lawyer–Trusts and Estates, Chicago, IL

For most people, law school will be a different educational experience from what they are used to. The expectations, level of competition, and teaching style will almost always be different from what you experienced as an undergrad. The key thing to remember is to be prepared, and prepare those around you for these changes. If you know what to expect, and are ready for it, you are capable of managing it. You are already off to a great start just by picking up this book and gathering experience from the many Voices of Experience who have been before you—remember to keep this focus on preparation throughout law school.

CHAPTER 4

Study Guidance

> "Preparing for the exam is different than preparing for the class. Reading, memorizing, and regurgitating information might have worked well in undergrad, but this studying technique is precisely what you want to avoid in law school. Exams are about application, and therefore the best way to prepare is to do practice tests and discuss hypothetical situations—remember that no two clients will have the same name—or the same problem!!"
>
> **–Law Student, Chicago, IL**

Law school is challenging academically and will require you to study religiously. The amount of work in law school can sometimes seem unmanageable, but it helps to remember that everyone else in your class is in the same boat. By the end of your first year, you will be amazed by your ability to read and absorb vast quantities of complex material. But of course, there is only one way to learn how to do this, and that is by doing.

There are also countless resources available to not only 1Ls but for you throughout your law school career. Be sure to use the first weeks of school to find your school's version of a study resource center. This is an area, at most schools, where you can check out various study guides. Often schools offer tutoring or small group sessions through their resource center as well.

"Either jump in all the way, or get out of the pool!"
—Law Student, Boston, MA

> *"I thought I studied in undergrad, but it was a joke compared with law school. I did not truly learn how to study until law school."*
> **–Lawyer–Medical Malpractice, Laveen, AZ**

DON'T FALL BEHIND IN YOUR READING

You will face an incredible amount of information in law school and it is easy to get overwhelmed by the sheer amount of material. It is easy to put off a reading or two until later in the semester. Resist this temptation! You will probably not have time to come back to material and if you fall behind it is very difficult to catch up. Jump in with both feet and hit the ground running.

You will learn the law by reading cases and discussing them in class. Rarely will you ever be definitively told "this is the rule of law" on a particular subject. You will have to extract this information from centuries of jurisprudence. This approach—which is called the *case method*—means you will have to read lots and lots of cases on a wide selection of subjects. As you move through your first year, and into your second and third, you will be able to significantly speed up your reading by learning how to spot key issues and facts while skimming cases. As you begin your learning, however, there is no substitute for reading each case thoroughly.

> "*When a professor assigns extra credit, assume that it is a required assignment. Not doing it will lower your grade. Don't underestimate the power of briefing your cases—it makes a huge difference in how you analyze the case and learn the law. If you have Internet access in class, don't use it. No one can play online poker and retain information from the lecture, no matter how smart you think you are.*"
> **–Lawyer–Trial Law, Valley Stream, NY**

"It is really true that you can't cram at the end for the exam. If you do, it is more likely than not that you will fail."

–Law Student, Washington, DC

"Don't rely too much on secondary materials. Let the organization of the casebook clue you in on what the point of each case is."

–Law Student, New York, NY

"Don't get too overwhelmed with the supplements. If you have one, that would be useful for the overall picture. Outline your classes or add on to an existing outline but don't waste too much time outlining. Practice tests will help you much more in your preparation."

–Lawyer–Civil Rights Law, Denver, CO

"*Just focus, get all of the work done on time, do not fall behind, keep up with the reading, and treat it as the only thing going on in your life. If you work very hard your first year, the next two years will seem a lot easier.*"

–Lawyer–Civil Rights Law, Traverse City, MI

"*Law school is a lot more about self-discipline than undergrad was. There were no quizzes, homework assignments, and quarter tests—so it takes a lot of effort on your own to keep on track.*"

–Lawyer–Business Law, Centreville, VA

"*It's like running a marathon. Keep it steady—reading a decent amount daily without falling behind.*"

–Law Student, Chicago, IL

"*I did not understand what it meant not to have a life in law school until the exam period during my first semester.*"

–Lawyer–Criminal Law, Forest Hills, NY

"I was told you can't cram for law school classes. Quite frankly, you can, it's just not the same as 'cramming' for undergrad classes. However, hindsight being 20/20, I probably should have put more effort into my classes. They are the foundation for the knowledge you need on the bar!"

–Lawyer–Legal Malpractice Law, Portland, OR

The Fact of the Matter

A recent study of law students found that 85 percent of 1Ls spend 20 or more hours per week studying. The study also found that 72 percent of 1L students were not working while in school. These rates change significantly in later years, with 70 percent of 2L students and 53 percent of 3L students spending over 20 hours per week studying. In line with this, and in contrast to 1L students, 45 percent of all law students are employed while in school.

(Source: LSSSE 2006 Annual Survey Results Overview, Engaging Legal Education: Moving Beyond the Status Quo, Law School Survey of Student Engagement, Indiana University Center for Postsecondary Research, www.lssse.iub.edu)

"*Do the work you're supposed to be doing starting in your first year and maintain that level of discipline for all three years. This means brief your cases, outline your notes right after class, obtain past exams, and do practice questions. This is really the ONLY way to not just get good grades but to really learn the material. The more you learn during law school, the less stressed out you'll be when studying for the bar exam. Get into the habit early so that you'll be prepared in the end.*"

–Lawyer–Trial Law, Arlington, VA

"*Do all of your work when you are supposed to do it. Do not fall behind on reading. This is important so that you get into the routine of keeping up with a schedule early on and do not learn bad habits such as procrastinating.*"

–Law Student, Philadelphia, PA

"*Do as much of the assigned reading as you can without driving yourself nuts. Don't stress yourself out too much and remember to take some time out for yourself. Figure out what works for you as far as studying goes and stick with it; don't listen to other students as much.*"

–Lawyer–Intellectual Property Law, London, U.K.

"*Do not, do not, DO NOT get behind on your reading! And when you do, catch up ASAP. Law school is like a box of Twinkies: you can't cram the whole thing down in a weekend . . . without consequences!*"

–Lawyer–Personal Injury, Barrington, IL

"*Regarding studying, treat it like a job: You put in your eight hours and you will get paid for eight hours; however, if you work 'overtime' not only will you get your regular pay, but you will also get 'time and half' if you go above and beyond.*"

–Law Student, Houston, TX

> *"Try to anticipate the volume of reading/
> work and forget any preconceived ideas as
> to any other classes previously taken."*
> **–Law Student, Dallas, TX**

> *"Try to learn as quickly as possible how to
> read cases for the important points of law
> and which facts led to the decision. Reading
> slowly, trying to absorb every last word of a
> case can be the death of the 1L. There is
> simply too much material to get through!"*
> **–Lawyer–Elder Law, Glendale, CA**

LAW SCHOOL: YOUR JOB

You will spend three years in law school
learning to be a lawyer. This is your job, and
it is best that you treat it as one. During your
first year, you will probably have to sign an
agreement that you will not work more than
15 hours per week. During the first year of

school, most students choose not to work at all. If you do need to work, consider a part-time program (which takes four years to complete). For almost all students, law school will leave little time to spend working. Remember, your three years in school is an investment in your future—better to put in all you can now and gain the rewards from this later.

"Undergrad helps prepare you for a full-time job. Law school is a full-time job."
–Law Student, Denver, CO

"Read, prepare, and relax . . . I treated law school like a 9–5 job my first year, studying my notes immediately after my classes and preparing for the next day. I was able to go into class and finals prepared and confident."
–Law Student, Miami, FL

" *Treat law school as if it were a job and put in the same amount of effort and hours you would as if you were working at a job and not in school.* **"**

–Lawyer–Intellectual Property Law,
Bessemer, AL

" *You have to be very dedicated and be prepared to work your tail off. Realize it's okay to stay in both weekend nights while your friends are at the bar because you have over 300 pages to read and brief by Monday.* **"**

–Law Student, Los Angeles, CA

" *People make a big deal about the 1L year, but your LIFE will be busy if you're going to be a lawyer, and you need to learn how to make room for priorities starting now.* **"**

–Law Student, Miami, FL

"*Law school is what you make of it. Some students study 60 hours a week and some study 10. If you just want to get by, you can get through with very little effort. Working at a part-time or full-time job will wreck your grades—so don't even try it!***"**

–Lawyer–Elder Law, Memphis, TN

WHAT ARE OUTLINES?

As mentioned earlier, law school will present you with an incredible amount of information to read, synthesize, organize, and remember. To help in this process, most students use outlines of legal concepts learned with relevant and important "case law" (translation: judicial decisions) noted. These are available commercially, and from other students, but—for most—there is no substitute for the learning process of making your own. To help you decide which approach will work best for you, try answering the following questions:

- Do you learn best from writing a concept and then reading it? If so, prepare your own outline as the process will do as much toward teaching you the concept as anything else.

- Do you learn best from reading the same concept over and over? If so, you can acquire an outline either from a study partner or other source.

Remember that there are often files of old outlines at your school in the study resource center. There are also numerous outlines available in the bookstore and from your peers.

> *"Don't be afraid to use outlines and outside preparatory materials. I remember thinking anything other than the book was somehow cheating, like reading the Cliffs Notes and not the book in high school. This is not true and outlines, as a supplement, are really helpful."*
>
> **—Law Student, San Francisco, CA**

"*Upperclassmen know what supplements to use and can give you firsthand information on how specific professors test. This information can help you tailor your studies.*"

–Lawyer–Trusts and Estates, North Hills, NY

"*Focus on reading the assignments and good note taking combined with focused review and outline construction. Stay away from commercial outlines. Synthesize the material yourself.*"

–Lawyer–Class Action Law, Lawrenceville, GA

"*Keep up with your class outlines. Take the necessary time at the end of each week (likely over the weekend) to complete the material you covered during the prior week.*"

–Law Student, San Francisco, CA

"*Resist the temptation to take shortcuts by using other people's outlines or blow off briefing cases. There will be times when you will have to prioritize, because there just isn't enough time to do everything. But it is always the best practice to make your outlines and keep up with briefing as best you can.*"

–Law Student, St. Louis, MO

"*For the most part, people are happy to share outlines, answer questions, and help out if they can.*"

–Lawyer–Litigation, Newark, NJ

"*Try to get outlines from upperclassmen who had your same professor.*"

–Lawyer–Business Law, Cerritos, CA

WHAT ARE STUDY GUIDES?

Study guides are as plentiful in law school as actual textbooks. You will get all kinds of advice from "don't use them" to "you can't live without them." Based on the number of study guides that your peers will purchase, it is likely that you will also fall into that camp. Ask some 2Ls or 3Ls which guides they prefer. You will likely find a brand that works well for your style. Very often if you sign up for a bar review course early in law school, you will receive study guides that help you throughout your law school career. These are often some of the best study guides for your first year.

One word of caution. Nothing substitutes for actually doing the reading. You can paralyze your learning by having too many study guides. Pick and purchase a few and stick with those. Buying everything on the market is not only costly but can lead to frustration and overload of an already tight time schedule.

❝ *Do what works for you in terms of studying—
be it flash cards, outlining, studying in
groups or alone, etc.* **❞**
  –Law Student, Boston, MA

❝ *Buy a PMBR, PLI, or other course
immediately (preferably one month before
classes start) and familiarize yourself with
all the outlines. Professors tend to hide the
law with convoluted reasoning.* **❞**
  –Law Student, Washington, DC

❝ *At the start of your first year, invest in
study guides so you spend time truly
learning the black letter law.* **❞**
  –Lawyer–Litigation, Louisville, KY

❝ *Read study guides and, most importantly,
take practice tests. In fact, take every single
practice test on the Internet, if you can.
Take Harvard's, Stanford's, University of
Chicago's, etc. Take them all!* **❞**
  –Law Student, New York, NY

"*Despite the fact that study guides are frowned upon in the first year, use them! If you do not come from a legal or government background, you will need a method to put all this new material into perspective. If you have the opportunity to take a pre-law school summer class, do it! I think the one major thing I regret is not having done this. I did not have the same background as most of my peers and I suffered as a result.*"

–Law Student, Dallas, TX

"*Do not concern yourself with the minutia of case law. Get a good commercial outline and learn the black letter Law. You will be much more efficient and be better prepared for your finals and the bar exam.*"

–Lawyer–Employment Law, Suamico, WI

> *"Bar review materials are really very helpful for first-year and for upper-level law school classes."*
>
> **–Lawyer–Business Law, Woodbury, NY**

> *"Don't be too embarrassed to use study aids or ask for help. You will need all of it you can get!"*
>
> **–Lawyer–Bankruptcy Law, Houston, TX**

> *"Look at all the bar prep materials at the onset, just to know what was coming and let it percolate in your brain for a couple years."*
>
> **–Law Student, San Francisco, CA**

SHOULD I JOIN A STUDY GROUP?

Simply put—you will want to find a study situation that works best for you. Many 1Ls find that study groups are a great way to improve their studying efficiency and better grasp complicated concepts. Study groups will form quickly in the first semester and will continue to reform as the year goes on. Here are some things you should consider in deciding what your study group looks like:

- Do you study best with one other person or a few other people?
- Do you do best in a group where you are the most talkative or where you listen more?
- Do you study best by being challenged by others? Or by reasoning through things?
- Do you do your best studying in the mornings, during the day, or late at night?

Your answers to these questions will help you determine not only the size of your study group but also the type of people you want in your group. Remember, there are plenty of people that decide they study best without a group and go it alone. There is nothing wrong with this style if it works for you.

"Listen to everyone, but believe only in yourself."
–Law Student, Baltimore, MD

"Do not listen to the people who tell you that they study 12 hours a day. Just do what you need to do to feel comfortable. I made two close friends and we studied for every exam together for three years. All three of us graduated near the top of the class."
–Lawyer–Intellectual Property Law, New York, NY

"*Focus on your own learning process. For many students, law school takes a little bit of time to click. Getting caught up in how other people are approaching their studies can be a distraction from figuring out your own method..*"

–Law Student, Los Angeles, CA

"*Don't be afraid to join a study group; you can learn a lot from your classmates . . . but choose wisely.*"

–Law Student, Chicago, IL

"*Get a good study group together with trustworthy people. Talk over your outlines and go to see the professors together with any questions.*"

–Lawyer–Mergers and Acquisitions, San Jose, CA

"*Get a study group or partner whom you learn well with. You may not have the same learning style as your best friend. Also, if you have not finished your own outlines within a week before the test, just use someone else's outline and memorize it. It's useless to spend the time making your own at that point.*"

–Lawyer–Class Action Law, Gilbert, SC

"*For the first year, I recommend that students join study groups with input from professors or upper level students giving emphasis on black letter law, not the minute details.*"

–Law Student, Chicago, IL

The Fact of the Matter
A 2006 study of relationships among law students found that 65 percent of students discussed ideas from their readings or classes with others outside of class (students, family members, co-workers, etc.), and 66 percent had serious conversations with students who are very different from themselves in terms of religious beliefs, political opinions, or personal values.

(Source: LSSSE 2006 Annual Survey Results Overview, Engaging Legal Education: Moving Beyond the Status Quo, Law School Survey of Student Engagement, Indiana University Center for Postsecondary Research, www.lssse.iub.edu)

"*Don't be too quick to choose a study group!!! First figure out your study habits and what works best for you … then find people with similar study habits and practices so that they can be a motivation to you as well as be of assistance to you when you want to discuss certain topics that you may be struggling with. For example, if you are the type of person to read a week ahead, then having a study group full of people that only stays on the current task won't help you at all. If you have questions about or want to discuss an upcoming lecture, they won't be able to discuss it with you because they haven't done the work yet!*"

–Lawyer–Trial Law, Winter Park, FL

"*Don't let other people's stress rub off on you. Just do the best you can do and don't worry about what anyone else is doing. Whatever works for your own study habits is the way to go, not what works for the person sitting next to you in class.*"

–Lawyer–Personal Injury, Dallas, TX

WHEN TO ASK FOR HELP

Law school will present you with an incredible amount of information—much of it new—to read and synthesize. Sometimes, a concept just will not click. It is important to realize two things. First, if it is not making sense to you, many other students probably don't understand it either! Second, you should speak up and get some insight on the subject. If you allow your question to go unanswered, you may never get a chance to come back to it or, worse, find that it is a foundation concept upon which other elements of law hinge. You are in law school to learn—don't be afraid to stop the process if something is not making sense.

"*Don't be afraid to ask questions. You will be exposed to many new concepts in law school, and you need to be able to comprehend those new concepts. If you don't understand something, ask for help. Chances are that there is someone else in class that needs help understanding the topic just like you. If the answer to your question is not in your textbook, find the answer elsewhere.*"

–Lawyer–Trial Law, Farmington Hills, MI

"*Try to find upperclassmen who are actually willing to sit down and give advice.*"

–Law Student, Dallas, TX

"*Ask questions! Seek out answers! Don't wait for things to be handed to you!*"

–Law Student, Philadelphia, PA

"*Be focused, study hard. Do not get discouraged. Reach out for help when you need it.*"

–Law Student, Los Angeles, CA

"*Do the reading before class, ask questions in class, and don't be afraid to meet the professors outside of class to clear up any other questions you may have.*"

–Lawyer–Class Action Law, San Francisco, CA

"*Visit your professors and ask them to clarify concepts that aren't clear—they expect you to.*"

–Lawyer–Elder Law, Annapolis, MD

REMEMBER: FOR MOST, 1L IS THE TOUGHEST

During law school, you will hear an expression that "the first year they scare you to death, the second year they work you to death, and the third year they bore you to death." While this will not be true for all students, there is an element of wisdom in the statement. The most difficult part of first year is the fact that you are trying to simultaneously absorb a new way of thinking and deal with a large volume of reading. Add this to the pressure created by wanting to do well, and unprepared students will be in a state of panic. While there will frequently be more reading in later years, most students will master the "way of thinking" about law following the first year. So, while you are facing a challenging year, know that it does get better for most. The key is not to get discouraged.

> " *In law school I finally learned to use my brain and it 'hurts' at the beginning.*"
> **–Lawyer–Civil Rights Law, Matthews, NC**

"*Don't bother letting them 'scare you to death' the first year. The key is to speak up whenever you think you know the answer—you won't get ridiculed if you're wrong, and volunteering cuts down the chance you will get called on when you don't know the answer.*"

   –Law Student, Boston, MA

Inside Tip

As you read your material for class, try to predict what components of the case the instructor will discuss in class. In time, you will find the ability to recognize these patterns will help you brief cases and prepare for exams.

"*Once you get past your first year, it's smooth-sailing, so hang in there.*"

   –Law Student, Sacramento, CA

"Be PATIENT. The learning curve is what it is. Just like learning a new language, it takes time to adjust. Stay FOCUSED. It's hard to do what's in front of you if you are distracted with emails from home about the dog running away or have credit collectors hounding you. Set boundaries with family, friends, and significant others about your time. DREAM BIG!!!"

–Lawyer–Intellectual Property Law, San Francisco, CA

"Tough it out. After the first semester, the stress gets a lot better. You will learn the best way for yourself to take notes, study for exams, take exams, and balance life with school. It just takes time, and once that happens things will fall into place."

–Lawyer–Business Law, Memphis, TN

"You will spend almost your entire first semester feeling stupid. Just trust that you are not, and things will eventually start coming together for you, and everyone else feels just as stupid as you do, even if they give what sound like brilliant answers (often lucky guesses) to the professor's questions."

–Law Student, New York, NY

"It only lasts three years. The first year is the most stressful, but it will pass. Students need to realize that they are in a room full of the best students, and their grades may not reflect their true knowledge."

–Law Student, San Diego, CA

"First year was definitely the hardest, that rumor is certainly not a lie, but I do find it's true that if you can get through that year, the rest is so much smoother."

–Lawyer–Litigation, Maspeth, NY

"*The workload doesn't get any easier (in fact, for some classes it will increase), you just get better at doing it. So where it might seem daunting to read 25–30 pages for your torts class first year; you'll learn not to bat an eye when your trademarks professor assigns you 45–50 pages for class during your second year.*"
–Law Student, Denver, CO

"*One of the keys to law school is never stopping—people don't make it because they give up when they get a few bad grades; but even if that happens—if you want it bad enough, you can do it. Believe in yourself!*"
–Law Student, Los Angeles, CA

Law school requires a lot of work as you strive to master the content and way of thinking necessary to become a great attorney. As the Voices of Experience indicate, there are a number of methods that can—and will—help you absorb and synthesize all of this information. At the end of the day, however, there will be no substitute for rolling up your sleeves and doing the work. If you can do it, try to work it so that this is all you have to do (at least during your first year)—the workload of school will be enough on its own!

CHAPTER 5

Grades and Standing

"As far as I know, law school finals haven't killed anyone ... yet."

—Lawyer–Trusts and Estates, Los Alamos, NM

This will come as no surprise, but grades are important at most law schools (gasp!). A handful of law schools use alternative scales, but most schools are A to F (don't worry too much—the latter are rare). At many schools, the average grade is a high C or low B. Like the other members of your class, you'll arrive at law school day one ready to do your best.

Some of you will "ace" everything and some will be frustrated. Most will fall in between.

> "I sailed through undergrad and made good grades. Law school required substantially more pre-class work and after-class review. In undergrad, there were midterm exams and other assignments that made up part of the semester grade. In law school, you gorge on information for 16 weeks then regurgitate that information in a three-hour exam. Your success in the course is based solely on one test, and, despite popular myth, the grade is not based on a professor's opinion of your writing, but is based fairly objectively on your ability to comprehend the fact pattern, identify the applicable rule of law, and apply one to the other to reach a logical and reasonable conclusion."
>
> **–Lawyer–Civil Rights Law, Brick, NJ**

IT'S ALL ABOUT THE FINAL EXAM

In most classes, there will be only one exam at the end of the semester, covering all the material learned, which will typically count for your entire grade. Exams are usually anonymous, although grades are often posted (by random number assigned before the test) following the exam. While some professors will credit you for in-class participation, it usually is not part of your grade.

" *Keep your eye on the prize. Only one day counts—the exam day. All your effort during the semester should be geared toward doing what prepares you to take the particular exam in the particular class for the particular professor.* "
–Law Student, Baltimore, MD

The Fact of the Matter

In numerous studies, the Law School Admissions Council has identified a meaningful correlation between students' LSAT score plus undergraduate GPA and performance during the first year of law school. This correlation has been reported at as high as 0.49.

(Source: *Beyond FYA: Analysis of the Utility of LSAT Scores and UGPA for Predicting Academic Success in Law School*, Linda F. Wightman. University of North Carolina at Greensboro, Law School Admission Council Research Report 99-05, July 2000)

"*It's not just about learning the material and regurgitating it on a final, it's about learning the material so that you can apply it to an entirely new situation that you've never seen before. Most people aren't prepared for that change their first semester and think that as long as they know the material they'll do well.*"

—Law Student, Houston, TX

"*Law school teaches you how to be a lawyer, not substantive law. In law school you can't cram for finals like you do in undergrad.*"

–Lawyer–Trial Law, Orlando, FL

"*Don't think about the grades. Grades are relative. Learn as much as you can and the grade will sort itself out. You can't control the mandatory curve or the distribution of grades so why worry about it?*"

–Law Student, Philadelphia, PA

"*Final exams as a 1L are not as bad as they seem. Take a deep breath and trust that you know the information. If you put the time in during the semester, it will pay off on the final exam.*"

–Law Student, San Francisco, CA

"No matter how hard you think you've studied during the school year, study like crazy for finals."

–Law Student, New York, NY

"Everyone knows the law come exam time, but not everyone can write about it under timed conditions and do so coherently. The students that can will succeed."

–Lawyer–Employment Law, Boulder, CO

"Talk to upperclassmen who have taken your professors. Talk outside of the classroom with every professor you have. Do practice exams in every subject before finals and go over it with the professor. There is no substitute for 'butt-in-chair' when it comes to studying (to quote my dean)."

–Lawyer–Legal Malpractice Law, Irvine, CA

FIRST SEMESTER AND 1L PERFORMANCE

Thinking and writing in the style that is expected is something that everyone will eventually master—but it does take longer for some than others, and this affects first semester grades. Performance for this first semester is important—it is the starting point for your GPA and will help you land jobs after your first year. You should do your best, but recognize that being number one is not everything.

> *First-year grades are the most important to getting a big firm job, if that interests you.*
> **–Law Student, Washington, DC**

> *Get serious about studying early. Grades after first semester can mean everything as far as recruiting opportunities later on.*
> **–Lawyer–Medical Malpractice, St. Louis, MO**

The Fact of the Matter

In a recent study of law school students, about 40 percent reported grades of either A/A– (18 percent) or B+ (25 percent); 29 percent of students reported mostly Bs. More than a quarter reported B– (15 percent), C+ (8 percent), or lower (5 percent) grades.

(Source: LSSSE 2006 Annual Survey Results, Engaging Legal Education: Moving Beyond the Status Quo, Law School Survey of Student Engagement, Indiana University Center for Postsecondary Research, www.lssse.iub.edu)

"Expect the unexpected. Law school is a fierce competition. You must learn and acquire the essential test-taking skills in order to do well your first semester, NOT just first year. The first semester is CRUCIAL because these grades determine your job prospects."

–Law Student, Miami, FL

" *Study REALLY hard and make law school one of your top priorities . . . if you can do well your first year, the rest will be much less stressful.* "

–Lawyer–Bankruptcy Law, New York, NY

" *Test yourself to see where you are weak in a particular subject. Work through mock exams. There are several available either online or in study aids available in the school bookstore. If you can't find one, make your own.* "

–Law Student, Dallas, TX

"*Just because a student seems to be vocal and confident in the classroom (i.e., being a 'talker'), it's those very same students who, generally speaking, are the ones who do not know what they are talking about and you will realize this by the end of the year. It's important to surround yourself with good people; likewise, align yourself with peers who seem committed to producing a good work product (if you're going to go the study-group route).*"

–Law Student, Chicago, IL

"*Don't get discouraged if you feel you aren't getting it. Nobody else is either, even if they sound like they do. Things will come together after the first year.*"

–Lawyer–Mergers and Acquisitions, Saint James, NY

"Don't stress out, it is only an exam . . . one grade will not make or break whether you become a lawyer. The person with the highest grades and the person with the lowest grades are both called lawyers after finishing law school."

–Lawyer–Real Estate Law, Oakdale, PA

"Do not second-guess yourself. Go with your gut feeling on exams."

–Lawyer–Mergers and Acquisitions, Oak Park, IL

"Even if your work is excellent, you could be a B–/C+ student your first year (depending on the curve set by your school). I'm glad someone prepared me for that."

–Law Student, Los Angeles, CA

GETTING TO THE TOP OF THE CLASS

Most law schools will have class standing, and many students will obsess about it. It is not unimportant—most large firms will look for the "top of the class" when hiring for summer positions. Consequently, competition is fierce to get to the top, and you should do your best to get there as it will open a lot of doors for you. Realize, however, that not everyone can, or will, be number one. It is not the end of the world if you do not make it to the very top. Give law school your best effort and work from there.

> "Get outside sources and start studying early in the semester. Figure out what kind of grades you want, because you have to put in hours of studying if you want to be at the top of the class."
>
> **–Lawyer–Mergers and Acquisitions, Blythewood, SC**

"Brief cases until you are blue in the face. It's the only way to get comfortable picking out the relevant issues from the dicta. While studying, do several practice exams and compare your answers to model answers if possible. You need to feel comfortable creating answers within a time constraint."

–Law Student, Chicago, IL

"Do as many practice questions as possible in the core subjects (i.e., torts, contracts, property). My first year I did not realize that there were practice supplements available, such as PMBR's finals series, and I did nothing but read the cases along with my class notes when preparing for my exams."

–Lawyer–Employment Law, Houston, TX

"*Go over old exams that the professors have on file. I had one professor who recycled an old exam, which I studied the day before I took the exam. Needless to say, I did very well in that course.*"

–Law Student, Boston, MA

"*Don't listen when people tell you that if you aren't in the top 5–10 percent you won't find a job. There are so many great firms out there outside of the big names that will provide you with an equal if not better experience and probably more hands-on experience. Take practical classes, clinics, trial advocacy, and others that are practical to the actual practice of law.*"

–Law Student, Washington, DC

"*STUDY, STUDY, STUDY. Law school is not college. When you look at the people in your law school section think this way: probably 60 percent of the class was in the top 10 percent of their college class. Realistically not everyone can be in the top 10 percent of law school. If you want to be in that top 10 percent you have to work harder than the rest of them.***"**
    –Lawyer–Business Law, Arlington, VA

"*Continuously review from the beginning— don't wait until exams are near. Seek clarification about a legal issue that you don't understand when it arises—don't expect it to resolve itself.***"**
    –Law Student, St. Louis, MO

"*Know the legal rules cold. Having this knowledge will serve you well on exams and it will make studying for the bar bearable.***"**
    –Law Student, New York, NY

"Definitely outline for your classes. It's more about the process than the actual outline— it was an amazing feeling when the whole picture came together every time I finished an outline. Definitely take as many practice exams as you can—this is vital!"

–Law Student, San Francisco, CA

"Don't spend too much time preparing for class by reading the cases in detail. Spend more time reviewing out of hornbooks and commercial outlines. This will improve your exam performance, which is what really matters in law school."

–Lawyer–Entertainment Law, New York, NY

"On test day, there are two very important rules: First, do not get to school early. The stress and the tension will psych you out; secondly, do not stay after to discuss the exam. When others discuss their performance it just makes you feel worse."

–Law Student, San Diego, CA

Inside Tip

Because the final is worth all (or almost all) of your grade for a course, it is worthwhile to focus on it early. Seek out past examples of exams that are available in the library and students who have had your professor for a subject to get an idea of what will be tested; it will help guide your preparation throughout the semester and as you approach the exam.

"In undergrad you were likely the star student—the A-type personality, the best of the bunch. Law school is a school for people just like you. You will have to fight to stand out. You'll have to work harder than anyone else to receive the same attention you received from professors with little to no work in undergrad. I know—that's depressing. The good news: Whether you graduate in the top 10 percent or the bottom 50 percent, you still graduate— you're still a lawyer—you'll still get a job!!"

–Lawyer–Environmental Law, Houston, TX

"You got great grades in college. So did everyone else in law school, but they have to curve the grades—so don't jump out your window over a B. Have a little perspective."

–Law Student, Dallas, TX

"Everyone in law school is accustomed to making As and being the top of their class. Law school is very different and As are few and far between."

–Lawyer–Real Estate Law, Jacksonville, FL

"Don't get discouraged. Everyone is stressed and frustrated. Just make sure you do everything you are supposed to. You cannot treat this like college by putting studying off until exam time. Study the material as you learn it!"

–Lawyer–Employment Law, Texarkana, TX

"Don't panic and establish a routine quickly. Don't get so lost in case law that you forget to study the black letter for exams."
–Lawyer–Bankruptcy Law, Highland, IN

LEGAL RESEARCH AND WRITING

During the first year, most students will have a class on legal research and writing. While this course does have grades, they are not typically given in the same way as other 1L courses (and at many schools, this course is pass/fail). In this class, you will learn some of the practical approaches to writing and researching like an attorney. For many students, this course is one of the most valuable you will take in law school as it can help with exam writing technique and teach you essential skills needed for your career as an attorney. Take this class seriously—the skills learned will benefit you for many years.

"*Pay a lot of attention in legal research and writing. You'll need to remember that stuff for the rest of your career.*"
–Lawyer–Trusts and Estates, Houston, TX

"*Going to law school is like learning how to read and write all over again. You may have been an excellent writer in college, but don't be discouraged when your legal research and writing papers come back dripping red ink . . . legal writing is a whole different ballgame.*"
–Law Student, New York, NY

"*Try and do all of your legal writing assignments in advance so you can spend the remaining time editing and sharpening your writing.*"
–Law Student, Philadelphia, PA

" *Take legal writing seriously. It might not count for much in the GPA, but all employers—particularly federal judges—will look closely at this grade. Also, legal research writing is your major job duty from 1L summer on, and it's important to learn how to do it well.* "
   –Lawyer–Elder Law, Lenexa, KS

" *Listen to your legal research professor, though it's boring, they have much needed information.* "
   –Lawyer–Mergers and Acquisitions, Warren, MI

" *Writing well is key not only to getting good grades on essay exams but also in being able to communicate well-organized and substantive thoughts.* "
   –Law Student, San Francisco, CA

Grades are undoubtedly an important part of law school and, as the Voices of Experience note, they are even more important during 1L. As you plan for your first year, weigh this need to perform well during first year against other obligations you may have in this time. Where possible, you should focus as much of your energy as possible to doing as well as you can. Throughout, don't forget that while getting to the top is a great goal, it does not need to define you as a person. Remember, it is something that, by definition, only a small group of students achieve.

CHAPTER 6

Beyond Grades: What Else Matters?

"Don't worry about getting involved. Too many people warned me about not having enough time for extracurriculars and I believed them. But I think it would have been better to be a part of organizations early so I could have built a better network/foundation."
–Law Student, Miami, FL

While the bulk of your time during first year will be spent focusing on your grades, you may also want to think about other opportunities to stand out from the crowd. While these activities should never take the place of focusing on your academic performance (and some are reserved for your second year of law school in part for this reason) it is worthwhile to think about what other activities are important in law school.

JOINING THE BAR

A number of states allow or even require you to sign up for the bar during your first year. While it is a time-consuming task to complete all the paper work, it is often required and saves you time on the backend. You likely know where you think you will practice law and, therefore, which bar exam you will be signing up to take. You can check on a state's specific requirements by going to the state board of law examiners website.

If your state does require you to sign up as a first year, be certain to do so as the financial penalty for not doing so is often great. In the cases where you are required to sign up as a first year, often law schools will offer on-site opportunities for the fingerprinting portion of the sign-up process. Be sure to watch the announcements at your school for this service. It is much easier to do this at your law school rather than traveling to your local police station.

AMERICAN BAR ASSOCIATION LAW STUDENT DIVISION

This is a relatively inexpensive organization to join and one that has numerous benefits and takes little of your time. When you join the ABA Law Student Division, you receive at least two publications, access to numerous online resources and Web boards, discounts on bar review programs, opportunities for leadership, and more. As a practicing attorney you will join the ABA, and as a law student the resources are large enough that this should be an easy decision for you! The website is www.abanet.org/lsd/home.html.

The ABA Law Student Division also offers student leadership positions and an annual conference. Many have found this to be a wonderful leadership and personal growth opportunity.

LAW REVIEW

Almost all law schools publish one or multiple student-edited law reviews, which are scholarly journals focusing on current legal issues. Being part of law review is probably the single most important and prestigious activity that you can engage in while in law school. Of course, as with everything else in law school, competition is fierce. Typically, several students are selected based on grades or class standing and others "write on." If you can, attempt to get on one—the effort will pay off.

" *Take legal writing and research classes very seriously. Don't just get by in that first-year class; that is what your summer jobs and post-grad positions will involve. Success in those classes opened many doors for me, including law review.* "

–Lawyer–Trial Law, Haslett, MI

The Fact of the Matter

As of November 2006, the LexisNexis Directory of Law Reviews listed 184 student-edited law journals and 320 specialty focus student-edited law journals at ABA approved law schools.

(Source: LexisNexis 2006 Directory of Law Reviews, compiled by Michael H. Hoffheimer, 2006 http://www.lexisnexis.com/lawschool/prodev/lawreview/default.asp)

"*While it may be miserable, bite the bullet and pour your heart and soul into your first year of law school. Whether it's right or wrong, top-level firms rely heavily on your grades, so excelling academically will open exponentially more doors for you in both jobs and academic honors groups like law review.*"

–Law Student, Chicago, IL

"*Between 1L and 2L the best thing to do is position yourself to get onto the law review or most prestigious journal at your school.*"

–Lawyer–Legal Malpractice Law, Bowie, MD

"*Keep up with the reading, as it pays off with opportunities for law review, moot court, job opportunities, and bar review.*"

–Law Student, San Antonio, TX

> *"1L is by far the most important year of law school. Your 1L grades determine what job you will get and what kind of opportunities you will have, such as making law review. So work hard and stay organized."*
> **–Lawyer–Real Estate Law, Providence, RI**

> *"If you are ambitious enough to want such accolades as law review and mock trial, then you better work hard and work smart your first semester; otherwise, you will spend the later two and a half years struggling and trying to make a name for yourself."*
> **–Lawyer–Personal Injury, Germantown, WI**

CLUBS AND OTHER ACTIVITIES

You are in law school with a small group of dedicated, smart students. It is only natural that many of them will form clubs and other organizations, many of them around social, political, and legal issues. Membership (and leadership) in these clubs can be a great way to connect with issues that interest you and build your résumé.

Join a few that are of great interest to you. Joining will broaden your perspective and also allow you to meet other students. Just remember, your studies and reading will need to come first and the amount of reading in law school takes some getting used to. You can always continue to join organizations later in law school.

> *Be sure to get involved with some extra-curricular activities at school. These activities will make you more invested in your school and allow you to network with faculty, administration, and fellow students.*
>
> **–Law Student, Houston, TX**

"*Be sure to find an older student in your school to advise you on what classes are good to take and which professors are better at helping you learn than others. They can also, in most cases, help provide you with outlines and advice on things going on in your school and what organizations to join.*"

–Lawyer–Employment Law, Ballwin, MO

"*Join clubs and organizations as soon as possible.*"

–Law Student, Boston, MA

"*Treat your first year of law school as a full-time job. Do not worry about getting involved with extracurriculars unless you find an activity that you are really interested in.*"

–Law Student, Los Angeles, CA

Inside Tip

Many law schools offer an orientation day where most clubs, organizations, and bar review companies are present. While it might seem overwhelming at the time, pick up information from every table that you see. The information will help you make good decisions in the coming months.

> *Get involved in as many organizations as you can and are interested in.*
>
> **–Lawyer–Personal Injury, Macon, GA**

> *In your first year of law school, your best connections will be other law students, professors, faculty, and staff at your law school. Explore clubs and committees, visit professors you connect with at their office hours, get to know the career center and the library staff, and check out the clinics on campus.*
>
> **–Law Student, San Francisco, CA**

Inside Tip
Actively seek out activities and organizations you want to be involved with. Law students tend to be proactive in looking for areas of interest and assume others are the same—don't expect great opportunities to come to you. Make the first move.

"Join clubs and activities. This was an easy way to meet people who had just finished 1L. As a result, I received invaluable advice, tips, and friendship."
–Law Student, New Orleans, LA

"Try going to clubs you are interested in and talk to the 3L and 2Ls. Many are happy to help 1Ls survive law school."
–Lawyer–Litigation, Houston, TX

❝*Join clubs and participate in clinics—not only are they great experiences, they are great for networking.*❞
–Lawyer–Class Action Law, Nashville, TN

MOOT COURT

The popular image of the practice of law is lawyers battling it out in the courtroom. While for most lawyers this is only a small part of the reality of practice, you will have a chance to practice in a mock courtroom while in law school. This is called "moot court." At most law schools, students will have the option to participate in moot court during their second year. Teams will compete and advance in standings until finals. It is a great challenge that is closely watched and a great résumé builder (particularly if you want to litigate).

"*Participating in activities, such as law review and moot court, will also make you attractive to summer employers.*"
    –Law Student, Philadelphia, PA

"*Professors who teach clinics, moot court, and other nontraditional classes can sometimes be more approachable than traditional professors.*"
    –Law Student, Chicago, IL

"*Get experience! I think I learned the most during my internship and moot court. I had to figure out how the legal system worked, and that is quite different from knowing the law.*"
    –Lawyer–Intellectual Property Law, New York, NY

> ❝*If you are in the top of your class, be prepared to become overwhelmed with the amount of 2L fall interviews that you do. Try to schedule your first semester of 2L to account for any interviewing and tryouts for trial team or moot court.*❞
> **–Lawyer–Real Estate Law, Redlands, CA**

INTERNSHIPS AND VOLUNTEER OPPORTUNITIES

Many students will have opportunities to do internships after their first year. Even before this, opportunities for volunteering abound in law school and are typically something that students do not take as much advantage of as they should. From legal clinics to pro bono organizations, many groups are eager to have help—even from first-year students. Overall, these present great opportunities to get some hands-on legal experience and meet practicing lawyers who may point you in the direction of a great summer (or full time) position.

"Plan to get some practical experience while you're in school—it makes a huge difference. Try to really figure out where you want to be when you graduate."
–Law Student, Dallas, TX

"Start preparing for legal careers by seeking out pro bono, volunteer, or clinical experiences while in law school."
–Lawyer–Civil Rights Law, Sunnyside, NY

"My school has a built-in mentor program, which is wonderful. I also suggest volunteering as a law student and doing pro bono work with practicing attorneys in areas that interest you. Also, join your local bar and other organizations."
–Lawyer–Product Liability Law, Chicago, IL

> *"Getting an internship or some extracurricular position/job will greatly enhance your marketability and likelihood that you will get a job after graduation."*
>
> **–Lawyer–Trusts and Estates, Spring Lake, MI**

> *"Choose your internship after your second year wisely. It will determine your career path."*
>
> **–Law Student, Washington, DC**

> *"Once you realize you are not in the top 10 percent of your class, get out there and start networking and looking for legal clerkships/internships. This is how everyone I know who wasn't in the top of the class found a job."*
>
> **–Lawyer–Personal Injury, Phoenix, AZ**

> *"Have mentors assist with studying methods, guidance, and even when looking for summer internships."*
>
> **–Law Student, Los Angeles, CA**

The Fact of the Matter

Below are the law school activities third-year students did (or planned to do) while in law school.

Volunteer or pro bono work	64%
Clinical internship or field experience	70%
Student-faculty committee	22%
Work on a legal research project with a faculty member outside of course or program requirements	30%
Study abroad	12%
Law journal member	26%
Moot court team	21%
Law student organization member	75%
Law student organization leader	47%

(Source: LSSSE 2006 Annual Survey Results Overview, Engaging Legal Education: Moving Beyond the Status Quo, Law School Survey of Student Engagement, Indiana University Center for Postsecondary Research, www.lssse.iub.edu. Results based on activities students indicated they had "Done" or "Planned to Do.")

"*Participate in the internships/externships your school provides—I met my most valuable mentors as my supervisors at my internship.*"

**–Lawyer–Mergers and Acquisitions,
Bala Cynwyd, PA**

"*Work as a research assistant, and volunteer for things like teaching assistant positions. Don't be overly concerned with law review or moot court . . . although nice on a résumé, they don't always get you a job.*"

–Law Student, Miami, FL

"*Volunteer somewhere. I guarantee that you'll be a better lawyer and a better person because of it.*"

–Law Student, Boston, MA

"*Be proactive in making contacts and landing that job or internship. Don't wait for a recruiter to come to you. Use your campus and community resources wisely.*"

–Lawyer–Trusts and Estates, Weaver, AL

"*I would advise getting legal experience if at all possible. It doesn't have to be a 'conventional' legal job and chances are it probably won't, but find out about doing a judicial externship through your school or volunteering with a public interest organization. These activities will allow you to get real hands-on legal experience that employers will look favorably upon.*"

–Lawyer–Bankruptcy Law, Flushing, NY

"*Always get a summer internship in the legal field. Any experience you can get during the summers is invaluable later on in your career.*"

–Law Student, New York, NY

"*You don't want to give up gaining relevant experience. If you do not need to take summer classes to graduate on time, then I suggest taking a summer clerkship/ internship. If you are one of those that already has everything set up for after graduation (job-wise), then take off and have fun over the summer.*"

–Law Student, New York, NY

"*Don't fret if you don't have a legal job over your first summer. If you can't get a paid internship, see if you can get a volunteer position (the DA's office will always take in unpaid law students).*"

**–Lawyer–Environmental Law,
Pembroke Pines, FL**

"Spend a few days in a law firm job shadowing. Many people have a false impression on how lawyers actually spend their time, and you don't want to go through three to four years of study and come out hating your profession. In fact, an internship or clerkship of some sort very early on in your law school career would be most beneficial."
—Law Student, San Diego, CA

And, most certainly, the resources to law students online are plentiful. There are study sites, advice sites, fun sites, blogging sites, and the list goes on.

Getting yourself involved in extracurricular activities can be a great way to gain valuable experience and contacts. While it is easy to only focus on the considerable amount of work and time needed to prepare for your classes, think about the recommendations made by the Voices of Experience as you start into your first year. You will have to put in additional effort for these activities, but the benefits will likely be significant both while in school and later in your career.

CHAPTER 7

Getting to Know the Faculty

"Talk to your professors! Despite every 1L's belief to the contrary, professors are human and many of them genuinely care about the students they teach."

–Law Student, Washington, DC

One of the most important things you can do as you enter into your first year is decide that you will spend time getting to know the faculty. Whether your undergraduate experience was at a small school that allowed you to get to know most of the faculty or at a very large school where you only were really able to get to know a few of your faculty members, remember that law school is a new opportunity to get connected. As you have seen in previous chapters, you will find yourself extremely busy your first semester. How will you find time to get to know the faculty? Make time. Go in during their office hours. Go in to talk with them before class starts. Go in to talk to them after class. Take advantage of faculty-lead study sessions. In addition to potentially providing valuable guidance on what will be covered in class, professors can also often steer you in the direction of jobs or other opportunities.

"*Don't be afraid to go to a professor's office hours to ask for help on substantive classes or in personal matters. Most professors know what first-year law students are going through and are willing to take time to give advice and are very willing to help in any way they can. Find someone who is involved in what you are interested in as well. This is a good way to find a common ground and get beyond the student/professor relationship, which can feel very impersonal at times.*"

–Lawyer–Business Law, New Orleans, LA

"*Don't be afraid or hesitant to approach a professor whom you feel is akin to you in personality, background, or areas of interest. Professors are inundated with students, but students only have so many professors. If you take the time to introduce yourself and get to know a professor, you will automatically build not only a good professional relationship but a good friendship as well.*"

–Law Student, Baltimore, MD

> ❝Do it! Build relationships with your professors early on!❞
>
> **–Lawyer–Bankruptcy Law, Baltimore, MD**

ARE THEY AS BAD AS THEY SAY?

Law professors are typically not the stuff of which movies are made. Yes, you may encounter an overworked and tired law professor, but you will find most of them are there to help students learn the law and become excellent practitioners. And remember that every one of your professors was, as some point, also a law student.

> ❝Don't be afraid of going to your professors for help and advice.❞
>
> **–Law Student, Dallas, TX**

> ❝Don't be afraid to approach professors. Most of them are in their profession because they genuinely do want to help students.❞
>
> **–Law Student, Chicago, IL**

The Fact of the Matter
In 2007, the student-faculty ratio at all ABA approved law schools in the country was 15:1.

(Source: Official Guide to ABA Approved Law Schools, LSAC and ABA, 2007)

"Find a teacher you identify with and seek them out. Maybe it is a professor you know likes an area of law you are interested in. Be a sponge, soak up whatever knowledge they can provide."
–Lawyer–Trusts and Estates, San Francisco, CA

"Get to know your professors. Chances are, they are very interesting people who have a lot to offer outside of the classroom. If you get to know them, your professors can give you guidance for both your law school career and your professional career."
–Law Student, Chicago, IL

> *"It's a myth that your teachers don't care. This is not true. My professors would bend over backward to help me with ANYTHING!"*
>
> **–Lawyer–Trial Law, Mount Carmel, PA**

> *"Not all professors are going to 'Paper Chase' you. Most are actually quite nice and as long as you tried to prepare, they will be patient with you."*
>
> **–Lawyer–Employment Law, Dearborn, MI**

MAKE YOURSELF KNOWN BUT NOT ANNOYING

There are some dos and don'ts when getting to know the faculty.

DO:
- Go with your questions preplanned. Know what you are going to ask.

- Respect their time. Office hours are not unlimited and you should go with a limited number of questions.

- Introduce yourself every time you go in. Professors have several classes of students and may not immediately recall your name.

- Ask for tips to better understand the law or the critical-thinking process.

- Ask for suggestions on study guides.

DON'T:
- Go to office hours in lieu of reading. Be up-to-speed on your current assignments when going to office hours.

- Go to the wrong professor. Respect their specialties and ask property professors property questions and contract professors contract questions.

- Overstay your welcome, or as said above, DO respect their time.

"*Don't brownnose faculty members, but try and befriend a few.*"
–Lawyer–Intellectual Property Law, Worcester, MA

"*Actually go to the professors office's and talk to them about life, the law, and anything else.*"
–Law Student, San Diego, CA

"*After a few months of 1L, seek out the professors that you enjoyed in class and strike up conversations with them about your concerns with the law and/or law school. Hopefully one of them will be receptive. Continue to nurture this relationship with more professional and occasionally personal questions/issues.*"
–Law Student, Denver, CO

Inside Tip
Take advantage of social opportunities that your law school offers where faculty are in attendance. The faculty who attend these events are clearly interested in getting to know the student body. This is a great opportunity to meet professors whose class you may not be in.

"Don't be dissuaded by a professor who doesn't seem like a mentor; there are others out there ... find them before it's too late!"
–Lawyer–Environmental Law, New Bern, NC

TRY TO AVOID BECOMING *INFAMOUS*

You will have questions about cases, questions about the law, questions about the nuances, and then even more questions. Read and use study guides and online resources as much as you can. Use the time you spend getting to know the faculty to answer the questions that are really stumping you, not to answer all your questions! You want to be someone the faculty smiles at in the hallway, not the person they dread seeing at the office door. Remember—just like you have other classes to plow through, they have other students to help.

> ❝Find a professor that fits your personality and glom onto her or him for your entire law school career.❞
> —Lawyer–Trusts and Estates, Brookline, MA

> ❝Feel free to speak with your professors. Some are more approachable than others, but this is like anything else in life some personalities get along better with each other.❞
> —Law Student, Los Angeles, CA

> "*I think law school was much easier in a lot of ways—I was just there to learn the law. I found professors very supportive and encouraging and am glad I got to know more of them than I did as an undergrad.*"
>
> **–Lawyer–Employment Law, Port Orange, FL**

> "*Treat professors like human beings— they love bright people. Enjoy their knowledge.*"
>
> **–Law Student, Miami, FL**

WHAT IS THE TRUE VALUE OF FACULTY RELATIONSHIPS?

The true value of faculty relationships goes beyond helping you better understand the class you are taking with them. These are people who can become your mentors over the next three years and in some cases throughout your career. There are many stories of faculty members later helping students find jobs. In fact, there are law students that later end up working in a firm with their former faculty. In addition, you will eventually need members of the faculty to help you with your personal recommendations as well as help you make decisions about offers you have. Remember—your professors are people who love the law, which is exactly what you have decided to study for the next three years.

> "Build a mentor relationship with several people in various areas of the law. Build relationships with successful, purposeful, experienced academics and practitioners alike. People who are cosmopolitan with a broad view of things."
> —Law Student, Philadelphia, PA

"It's difficult to gain a mentor in your first year because the professor is teaching a large class, which may involve areas you don't enjoy. If you like a professor, take time to go to their office hours. Even if they don't specialize in your field of interest, they can point you to someone who is, and a good impression is invaluable when other faculty ask about you."

–Lawyer–Entertainment Law, Hoboken, NJ

"Definitely get a mentor. Many professors have internship and job contacts. It is so important."

–Law Student, Houston, TX

"Talk to professors. Your first year of law school is critical to forming relationships with people who will be credible references and recommenders, as well as people with insight into job availability and priceless advice."

–Law Student, Boston, MA

"*Find a professor you have something in common with. I became very close to two professors—one who was the advisor for my trial team and one who is a family law professor. These are the two areas I will be working in after the bar exam.*"

–Law Student, San Francisco, CA

"*Get involved in the activities that interest you—whether it's mock trial, pro bono, or the Business Law Society—and you will naturally find some older students, professors, or practicing attorneys who you can develop relationships with. In my experience, this works much better than school-sponsored mentorship programs, which are well-intentioned but match you up with people strictly by geography, which is usually not a good fit.*"

–Lawyer–Legal Malpractice Law, Washington, DC

"*Don't forget how important these relationships will be for recommendations for jobs and judicial clerkships. It is so important not to forget the big picture while you're struggling in your first year. Take opportunities to make yourself known to faculty in a good way and build relationships. Even if you aren't a top student, if you've built a good relationship and the faculty knows your personality, they can write a better recommendation letter for you. Go to events where faculty will be and mingle, go to their office hours and make a good impression in class.*"

–Lawyer–Real Estate Law, Washington, DC

> **The Fact of the Matter**
> In a 2006 study of law students, 73 percent indicated they found the quality of relationships with faculty members to be better than average at their schools. Fully 47 percent rated their faculty in the top two categories with regard to being "Available, Helpful and Sympathetic."

(Source: LSSSE 2006 Annual Survey Results, Engaging Legal Education: Moving Beyond the Status Quo, Law School Survey of Student Engagement, Indiana University Center for Postsecondary Research, www.lssse.iub.edu)

"Find a mentor that you admire for reasons that have nothing do with law school. Sometimes you find a professor that you really love who teaches a class in an area of law that never interested you and it opens you up to something new. Maybe you went to law school thinking you wanted to be a hot shot defense attorney but you have that one professor that sells you on family law so you decide to work for legal aid handling child custody cases."

–Lawyer–Litigation, Wilmington, NC

"*Having a mentor is both invaluable and absolutely necessary. You cannot do well in law school completely on your own, no matter what you think. You need help along the way and there's no one better to offer you such help than someone who has been in your shoes in the not-so-distant past. Take advantage of that by learning from their mistakes and take the advice they wish they had listened to. Most of all, don't forget to give back for everything you receive. The best way to thank your mentor is to serve as one yourself whenever you get the chance.*"

–Law Student, Dallas, TX

"*Check out the vitae, background, and publications of a particular professor you admire. If some specific area gets your interest and you want to build your knowledge base, approach the professor. Sometimes talking to one person leads us to other people.*"

–Law Student, St. Louis, MO

> *"In my first year, I was too busy just getting my feet wet with legal education. During your second year, you will learn more about your real interest in law, and you will develop the abilities to have a more engaging discussion with your professor. It will be natural to develop a mentor relationship at that time, too."*
> **—Law Student, Sacramento, CA**

You will find that, as in other areas of life, law school relationships are extremely important. There are many opportunities to get to know law school faculty, although many first-year law students do not take advantage of them. Where you can, go to office hours and study sessions with faculty. Take opportunities to ask questions and improve upon your understanding of the law. Create opportunities to get to know the faculty and understand more about the practice of law, the profession of teaching law, and the legal community in your area as well. Get to know the faculty sponsors of various organizations that you check out in your first year. Your future as a practicing attorney will be filled with relationships, and your law school faculty relationships are a great beginning.

Getting to know your fellow classmates in law school is inevitable. Forming lasting relationships with them is truly a bonus. The relationships you form will be valuable during law school and during your future practice of law. You will have the opportunity to study with and work alongside a number of your classmates. In addition, you will get to know their style, their thinking, and their work ethic plus who you like and who you would rather not spend much time with. Finally, you will learn who stretches your thinking skills in different ways. One thing is almost for certain—you will grow and learn from those around you. Getting to know those you will spend the next three years with is an opportunity that starts day one and is very important. Remember, you are forming lasting relationships that become even more valuable as you graduate, pass the bar, and dive into the profession of law.

CHAPTER 8

Choosing a Field

"Find several lawyers in different fields and follow them around for a day. Different lawyers perform a myriad of different tasks. Remember that not all lawyers receive that six-figure starting salary. It's not about the money. It's about waking up and desiring to go to work because you've found your passion."

–Lawyer–Trial Law, Panama City Beach, FL

You might be starting school knowing that you are going to be an entertainment lawyer, an environmental lawyer, or—as many think—a trial lawyer. Or you may be starting law school to see what you want to do next.

Whatever the plan, do yourself a favor and keep your mind, and options, open. You will be exposed to much in your first year that might help develop your career plan. You may find that corporate law is your one true love. Many a practicing lawyer will tell you they are not in the area of law they first thought they would be. And rest assured, while you will definitely be busy during your first year of law school, choosing your field is not something you have to accomplish as a 1L.

WHAT SUBJECTS DO YOU LIKE?

As you are exposed to new areas of the law, you will most likely find yourself enjoying certain classes more than other. While some of this will have to do with your professor, you will also see that you are more naturally interested and inclined toward certain areas of the law. There are several questions you can ask yourself as you start to decide which subjects you like more than others.

- Do you enjoy reading one hornbook more than others?
- Do you find yourself thinking about specific rules of law and wondering how they play out in practice?
- Do you find yourself doing extra research on a certain area of the law?
- Do you find yourself reading more than one study guide for a certain subject?
- Do you volunteer to talk more in some classes than others?
- Do some subjects seem to come much more easily for you?

WHAT PRACTICES DO YOU ENJOY?

Again, there are practices of the law that are more appealing to some than others. You will start to see along the way that you are more attracted to some things than to others. Start to notice your own preferences. You may be a great orator or you may find that research is extremely appealing to you. Again, there are questions you can ask yourself:

- Do you enjoy orally discussing a case more than briefing it?
- Do you enjoy writing all about the law more than you do speaking about it?
- Do you find yourself enjoying the specifics of contracts or commercial law more than the intricacies of torts?
- Do you imagine yourself working to change or champion a certain set of laws?

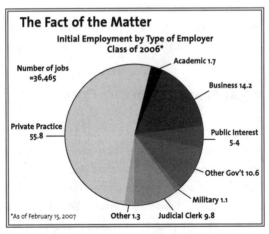

The Fact of the Matter

Initial Employment by Type of Employer
Class of 2006*

Number of jobs
=36,465

Academic 1.7

Business 14.2

Private Practice
55.8

Public Interest
5.4

Other Gov't 10.6

Military 1.1

Other 1.3   Judicial Clerk 9.8

*As of February 15, 2007

(Source: National Association for Legal Career Professionals, Class of 2006 Selected Findings, 2007—http://www.nalp.org/assets/768_classof06selectedfindings.pdf)

WHAT ELSE CAN YOU DO?

You should allow yourself opportunities to explore the areas of practice that interest you prior to working. Volunteer over spring break, shadow attorneys that you know, attend court. Ask upperclassmen what opportunities they have taken advantage of during their law school experience. Ask in your career services office about opportunities. They often have the inside track and more importantly, the early heads-up on what opportunities are available in the local community. Specifically, you should look for opportunities to observe lawyers in action to see if you would enjoy that area of practice.

"*Clerk or work in a law firm during the entire time that you are in law school.*"
–Lawyer–Bankruptcy Law, Minneapolis, MN

"*Talk to lawyers. The legal profession is very paternalistic. Make sure you know what you face as far as getting a job. It's all about connections, and if you don't have them, it's still possible to break into the legal profession, but it's much, much harder.*"

–Law Student, Portland, OR

"*Seek out professors who teach in the area of law that you are interested in. Establish these relationships early.*"

–Law Student, San Francisco, CA

"*Try to connect with a professor in an area of law you're interested in, and do a work-study or nonclass project with them to get a good reference in the field of law where you want to practice.*"

–Lawyer–Employment Law, Staten Island, NY

"*I would encourage more students to enter national writing competitions on a subject they like. Find a professor who likes the subject you want to write about and do a supervised research project. Get credit and possibly money. Work hard, show your interest, and you might get a letter of recommendation as well.*"

   –Law Student, Los Angeles, CA

"*If you know what type of law you'd like to pursue, take steps toward obtaining a job in that field. If you don't, try to intern with a judge who hears many different types of cases to gain some broader experience. Obviously 2L summer is more important than 1L summer, so you might use your 1L summer to do something law-related in an area that you're interested in but don't know much about.*"

   –Law Student, San Antonio, TX

"*If your professors have an open door policy (as mine did), use it! If not, identify people in your life or at work that are in the field you want to pursue and let them know that you want to work with them.*"

–Lawyer–Intellectual Property Law, South San Francisco, CA

"*It's good to have a mentor, especially in the field in which you want to practice, as well as in the location where you would like to practice so they can help you network early on.*"

–Law Student, New York, NY

"*My school offered a mentor program with practicing attorneys. I didn't find it helpful because I personally didn't know what kind of law I wanted to pursue and after some time with my mentor, I realized I wasn't interested in the kind of law she was practicing; consequently, our relationship dwindled. The best unofficial mentoring I received was from upperclassmen who I met through participation in student organizations. They can tell you what professors to take, or not take. They can give you job-searching advice, and they can give you a realistic expectation about what the next year will bring.*"
   –Law Student, San Diego, CA

"*Reach out to friends and family. Networking is an enormous part of success in the legal field.*"
   –Lawyer–Real Estate Law, Central Islip, NY

" *Professors are often the best mentors in terms of academics and helping you land a job. Pick someone you trust and stick with him or her.* "

–Law Student, Baltimore, MD

" *Pair up with upperclassmen and also with professors. Your professors especially have a lot of untapped resources for getting jobs and general law school career advice.* "

–Lawyer–Environmental Law, South Euclid, OH

The Fact of the Matter

In 2007, 89 percent of graduates from ABA approved law schools were employed nine months after graduation. At many top schools, this number is even higher.

(Source: Official Guide to ABA Approved Law Schools, LSAC and ABA, 2007)

"*Have lunches, coffees, and other meetings with any and all attorneys who are willing. Learn about different areas of the law.*"
–Lawyer–Intellectual Property Law, Pickens, SC

"*I think mentors are essential in two main areas: helping students navigate the stress and expectations of the first year, and providing advice on course selection for particular fields.*"
–Law Student, Chicago, IL

"*I had a few student mentors who I would call a few times a semester. They made me feel better when I would freak out and assured me that I would get everything done and be fine, which always provided a sense of relief. It is also great to have a few adult, teacher, or employer mentors to help you with the hard decisions that you will make throughout law school like summer employment suggestions, finding jobs, choosing between jobs, and things that will improve your legal career for the long term.*"
–Law Student, Washington, DC

"For law school in general, I would recommend that students go to the courthouse once or twice and watch various trials if they haven't done so already."

—Lawyer—Legal Malpractice Law, Chicago, IL

Inside Tip

Use your first year to volunteer and do as many "shadowings" as you can. Make it your personal quest to expose yourself to as many different legal fields as possible. Even just as an observer. Try things you don't think will interest you as well as those that are most intriguing to you. Never again will your plate be so wide open. Seize and enjoy the opportunity.

"Go to court. See as much as you can procedurally to get an idea of what things look like."

—Law Student, Boston, MA

"If you're looking for summer employment, look for jobs in the city you plan on working in after graduation. Keep an open mind about what kind of work you will consider doing—you never know when you might end up loving a certain type of law you swore you'd never practice."
–Law Student, New York, NY

"Even the bottom of the class gets jobs. Don't freak out about grades and class standing. Don't listen to negative talk."
–Lawyer–Product Liability Law, Ozark, MO

"*If you find a professor or dean in your school that you particularly like or respect, then make an effort to get to know them a little better. You don't have to have some deep question about class material either. I've found that one of the best ways to get to know a professor or dean is to ask for advice, whether it is about studying, your life in law school, or your career. This will help you cope better and will give you great recommendations if and when you need them for the job application process!*"

–Lawyer–Legal Malpractice Law,
   Washington, DC

Start law school with an open mind and work hard to keep an open mind at least in your first year. Your thinking about the law and about everyday occurrences will change during the three years you are in law school. It is likely that the area of law you are interested in may also change. You may even decide that law school and a legal education is great, but the practice of law does not particularly interest you. If this is the case, you will start to explore the myriad nontraditional areas in which attorneys work. Even if the area of law you wish to practice does not change, law school is the best opportunity to explore different fields.

CHAPTER 9

Law School Summers

"*During your 1L summer, pursue not what career services recommends you do, but what you yourself would like to experience. If you are pretty sure you want to work in a firm, but were always curious about diplomacy, work in an embassy to make sure you are on the right path. On the other hand, if you are pretty sure you don't want to work in a firm, you might want to try one out for half of your 1L summer, just to make sure. For the second half of the summer, do what you love. In the end, always do what you love, not what others tell you that you should love.*"

–Law Student, Denver, CO

Summers during law school are not unlike summers during undergrad. You can decide to not focus on the law and enjoy a less stressful summer. You can use the summer to take classes to get ahead and take classes for a joint degree or even take the summer to study abroad. Or you can decide to seek out and take a position that exposes you further to various practices of law. Like most aspects of law school, the advice is varied and the decision is one you should make based on your own situation.

That said, most employers would encourage you to start your legal career by seeking internships, externships, clerkships, and summer legal opportunities. Common wisdom would encourage you to use the summers to get your foot in the door of firms that are appealing to you. Look for jobs in the locale in which you wish to ultimately practice. Seek positions in areas that are interesting to you. Seek opportunities that allow you to gain experience that leads you to landing the dream job. It is certainly an added benefit that those that are "living on loans" enjoy the money made from summer opportunities.

"Find something that will give you both employment experience and fun, if possible. Do the study abroad that will give you travel, class credit, and experience. Do now what you are not going to have the flexibility to do once you graduate and use it as a chance to narrow down what you do and do not like in different legal fields."
–Law Student, Philadelphia, PA

"Get experience in and around the courtroom and justice system. This instills some common knowledge that will help you understand the subject matter of future classes and bar exam."
–Lawyer–Environmental Law, New York, NY

"Start actively searching for a job in the geographic location where you want to end up. It is very difficult to find a job in a location other than where you went to law school."
–Law Student, Boston, MA

LANDING THE DREAM JOB

You have defined your dream job or at least have an idea of what it will look like. Now, how do you land it? Successfully landing the dream job often requires strong grades, persistence, and most important, experience. What better time to get experience than while in law school? Make certain that you consider internships, externships, volunteer hours, and clerkships.

> "Although they say to relax and regroup that first summer, I would suggest starting to explore. The longer you wait to explore different types of law, or gain experience, the harder it is to catch up later. You cannot get that time back."
>
> **–Lawyer–Environmental Law, Cincinnati, OH**

> "Anything you can do that is law related is a plus—even if it is unpaid, it will look great on your résumé."
>
> **–Law Student, Dallas, TX**

"Do something fun, but make sure you also do something in the legal field, even if it's volunteer work. It's essential to have something on your résumé to catch employers' eyes in the fall of your 2L year, and to have something to talk about in your interviews down the road."

–Law Student, San Francisco, CA

"Ask a firm to do a free 'externship.' The experience will be invaluable for you. Being 'free' is great for the firm. You may even be able to get credits from your school."

–Lawyer–Class Action Law, Downers Grove, IL

" *Do something law related—period.
I made the mistake of going back to my
accounting firm and it made a difference
in my job hunt as a 2L. Even if you need
to volunteer, work for a judge or local
neighborhood legal services office. In
addition, you may want to take a class to
lighten your load later as a 3L, so you can
focus on working and gaining full-time
employment for after the bar.* "

–Law Student, Washington, DC

" *Do what you want and need to do, not
what everyone else is doing or tells you to
do. I chose to work pro bono after my 1L
year and take summer school so that I
could complete a dual degree program
instead of taking a paying job. People in
my class told me I should take a paying
job, but by taking summer school and
working pro bono, not only did I get work
experience, but I was also able to complete
what was supposed to be a four-year dual
degree in three years!* "

–Lawyer–Product Liability Law, Dalton, GA

"*My biggest regret was taking my 1L summer off, because I had friends that took classes all the way through and they were lawyers already by the time I was getting ready to graduate. Also, if you have any ambition whatsoever to work in a large law firm, you need to make it your mission to become a summer associate.*"

–Lawyer–Medical Malpractice, Chattanooga, TN

"*Always work a legal job in the summer. I don't agree when people say that you need not work a legal job the summer after first year. If I were an employer, I'd be more likely to hire someone that has two years of summer work experience in the field of law.*"

–Law Student, Miami, FL

"Get the best grades possible in your first year. These are almost the only grades that count—even if they tell you they are "advisory" grades. The employers will ask to see the grades. These grades will determine who gets the jobs at the end of your second year. The second-year job usually determines your job after graduation."

–Lawyer–Legal Malpractice Law, Seminole, FL

"Do something creative, if at all possible, where you will write or take a strong leadership role. My unique summer job (drafting biosafety protocols and preparing for a Centers for Disease Control plant approval) between 1L and 2L ended up landing me much better 2L summer offers than my class rank alone would have produced."

–Law Student, Chicago, IL

"*Do something exploratory. Most people view their job between 2L and 3L year as the one that will transition into a permanent job after graduation, but the 1L/2L summer is the time where you should explore. Go study abroad, or take a class or two or do something in a legal field that interests you. It really helps to do something where you can try to narrow down what kind of law you may be interested in, especially if you can do so in a law-pressure environment.*"

–Law Student, Dallas, TX

"*A summer associate position is critical to establishing working relations in the field.*"

–Law Student, New Orleans, LA

"*Do not consider leisure activities unless you have gained some form of practical experience in the legal field. Do not fail to engage in some practical legal experience (even if it's unpaid!).*"

–Lawyer–Product Liability Law, Braintree, MA

"*Balance between fun and work. These are the last two summers you will ever have. That said, try and get any kind of real-world lawyering experience, even if you have to intern at a law firm or shadow a judge for no pay and wait tables for money. Additionally, network, network, network. Getting a summer job in some states, especially when dealing with medium- and small-sized firms, is 10 percent grades and 90 percent who you know.*"

–Law Student, Miami, FL

"*Accept the fact that a good summer job is hard to come by after your 1L year, especially if you're in an area with a lot of law schools like Boston or New York. Try to do a mixture of the two and go for the experience over the paycheck. You'll have a lot more to talk about during your 2L interviews.*"

–Law Student, Minneapolis, MN

CAREER SERVICE OFFICES

The career service office at your law school
has a wealth of information and opportunities
for all law students. It is important that
you avail yourself of this resource early on
in your law school career. Get to know the
person who runs this office. Get to know the
job-posting system in use at your law school.
Get to know the workshops offered and make
the time to take advantage of them. Know
when to sign up for on-campus interviewing.
Be ahead of the process and this resource
will serve you very well.

And don't forget about on-campus recruiting.
Firms, corporations, and the government
come to campus with one distinct purpose—
to hire law students from that school. This is
your best opportunity. Take advantage of it.
Often career offices offer interviewing workshops. Take advantage of these as well. These
workshops can only serve to make you better.
Interview all you can as the experience is

good whether or not you end up in the job. Research those interviewing on campus and recognize they would not be there if they did not have positions available. Research the positions they have available. Ask your questions and use this as a process to determine your top picks for summer employment.

" First, be VERY NICE to the staff at the career services office; then apply for EVERY position you are interested in. This includes positions for which you may not qualify for because of class ranking or GPA. "
–Lawyer–Personal Injury, Austin, TX

" Go through on-campus interviews and take advantage of your career services office! Befriend the career counselors because if they know you personally, they're much more likely to go to bat for you with a prospective employer and to keep an eye out for any potential openings. "
–Lawyer–Trial Law, Chandler, AZ

"*Visit the law school's career services center; go to events that are offered at the law school. You will meet practitioners and alumni that can offer great advice and can be helpful during law school and post-law school.*"

–Law Student, Chicago, IL

"*Talk to a counselor at your school. They know what they are doing!*"

–Lawyer–Civil Rights Law, Savannah, GA

"*Career services and student affairs are there to help you, but be a grown up, and do your part by actively participating in their services.*"

–Law Student, Washington, DC

> ❝ *I got to know the dean of career services and I think that helped out immensely in my job search. I did not feel that forming relationships with professors was necessary.* ❞
> **–Lawyer–Class Action Law, Encino, CA**

> ❝ *Network early and often. As soon as you can, look into internships for the summer after 1L; go to career services and work with them closely.* ❞
> **–Law Student, Los Angeles, CA**

1L SUMMER VS. 2L SUMMER JOBS

Summer jobs after 1L are not expected at most law schools. They are a great opportunity to try out a firm that you don't know much about. Your 1L summer is a great opportunity to volunteer. As mentioned, some law students decide not to pursue a legal position or legal volunteer hours after their first year but instead do something completely unrelated. Many recent law school graduates even suggested this is a great time to go abroad. By your 2L summer you will want to focus on those places that you wish to receive an offer from. You should carefully select the one or two locations that you work at for your 2L summer. It is often your 2L summer job that turns into your first job.

"Research, research, research and be willing to work for free if it will help get you into the job that you want eventually. Working your 1L year is essential because it helps put the past year of law school into real-life focus. Working your 2L year is expected, but not quite as enjoyable since you are stressed about getting an offer."

–Lawyer–Elder Law, Birmingham, AL

"*Depending on the caliber of prestige your law school holds, I would say it is a judgment call. If you are going to have to claw your way to the top because your grades are poor or your law school does not have an abundance of on-campus recruiting, then it is probably a good idea to have some experience to put on your résumé.*"

–Law Student, New Orleans, LA

"*First year is exhausting and you will want to enjoy your summer so try to work at a firm with good hours, for example, any governmental agency, the state's attorney's office, or a local municipality.*"

–Lawyer–Litigation, Paris, France

> *"If you are not taking classes over the summer enjoy yourself as much as you can and use that time to engage in volunteer law-related or paid law-related jobs. Work on your connections for your future externship."*
> **–Lawyer–Class Action Law, Wichita Falls, TX**

> *"Paying jobs are difficult to find, and the ones that do come around often pay disappointingly low wages. Try to find something interesting—make sure it is law-related—and accept your first summer as a learning experience."*
> **–Law Student, New York, NY**

"*I took a position as a research assistant with a professor; I ended up having a great summer because I could, for the most part, make my own hours. Most weeks I only had three days of work that required me to be in a specific location, and beyond that, I could do the rest of my work from whatever vacation spot I might find myself in.*"

–Lawyer–Appeals Law, Riverside, CA

"*Begin your networking and begin to lay a foundation for name recognition. The first summer you want people to have seen you somewhere or recognize your name and you want to be able to do the same for judges, lawyers, staff, and others in your legal community. For 2L summer, I don't think you can begin to set up your summer plans too early in the year. If you can secure a position before the on-campus interviewing, then do that.*"

–Law Student, New York, NY

"*Split summer between two jobs. Work or volunteer in unrelated fields to discover what type of law interests you, or go to a summer abroad program and work or volunteer when you get back. Summer abroad is an opportunity that won't come back around and is an easy A.*"
   –Law Student, Houston, TX

"*This is your opportunity to be a little bit experimental. Definitely do work or an academic program somewhere (I recommend work, especially if you have never done legal-related work before), but it's a chance to try something nonstandard or work in a field you may not ultimately want to work in. Unless you already know exactly what you want to do. In that case, work in that field, to demonstrate interest, to make connections, and possibly to set yourself up for employment. The sooner you can work to angle for a job the better.*"
   –Lawyer–Trusts and Estates, New York, NY

" *The first year should be something you love to do (e.g., travel, study abroad, unique legal experience, etc.). The second year should be something you will hope to do upon graduation.* "

–Law Student, Philadelphia, PA

" *Choose a job carefully. If taking a job, pick one that provides actual legal experience, not just an opportunity to watch lawyers work. If taking summer classes, choose classes that lay a foundation for future law school or bar exam classes.* "

–Law Student, Houston, TX

" *If the students choose a study abroad class, the students should try to find substantive programs that are not glorified European or Hawaiian vacations. It is a crucial summer before on-campus interviews, and the right choices can help students stand out to employers.* "

–Lawyer–Criminal Law, Redding, CT

"*Do something both fun and interesting 1L summer because it's your only time to do so and it makes for great interview chat in the fall. Oh, and apply early, early, early.*"

—Lawyer–Real Estate Law, Torrance, CA

"*For summer after your first year, getting a job is EASY. Some people stress out about it, but they aren't approaching it correctly. First, you need to realize that you will probably not get paid. Once you get that, realize that you are offering a service for FREE to anyone willing to take you up on your offer. Most government and nonprofit legal associations do not have formal summer programs. (Of course, DA's offices in large cities and most federal government offices do have formal programs.) If you are in a big city, find the next closest DA, or public defender. Or the office in your hometown. Google something you are interested in like "Legal Services for Children." Find an agency you want to work for. They all have contact information on their website. Call or email them and offer them your free services.*"

—Law Student, Los Angeles, CA

WHERE TO LOOK

Start at school. Use the campus career office to determine who is recruiting with on-campus interviews. Also look to see who is posting jobs on campus even if they are not actively interviewing on campus. Utilize the network of alumni at your school. See where they are employed and call them for an informational interview if their position or their firm interests you. Talk to upper-classmen about where they have worked and if they know of any open positions. If you have identified a specific firm, corporation, or organization that you want to work for, call the hiring manager and ask if any positions are available. If need be, offer to do volunteer hours to gain the experience of working in their office.

" *You must take a proactive approach and network yourself outside of all law school networking functions. Why be a piece of paper in a stack of 200 applications when you can be a voice over the phone, talking directly to an attorney?* "

–Lawyer–Personal Injury, New York, NY

Inside Tip

Start early looking for your summer opportunity. Positions are most plentiful early in the semester. It is never too early to start seeking out and lining up the opportunities that are most interesting to you. Ask upperclassmen about their summer positions and follow up on interesting ones.

" *Find a job in an area of law you're interested in, but have little practical experience with. This exposure is priceless and don't worry if it's paid or not. Use those three months to build your résumé and build your understanding of different areas of the law that interest you.* "

–Lawyer–Product Liability Law, Haverhill, MA

" *For the job search, start early, and utilize as many connections that you can via family, friends, but most importantly the law school. Most law schools have extensive network connections that enable students to meet alumni working in their desired practice area, and these may lead to potential job offerings.* "

–Law Student, San Francisco, CA

" *Many will probably disagree, but don't be afraid to change your mind if you've taken an offer somewhere and then something better comes up. You have to make the best choice for your career, lifestyle, family, health, and overall well-being. Reneging on an offer for a summer position is easier than making a career firm change after several of years at an office, so make the change sooner rather than later.* "

   –Lawyer–Employment Law, Portland, OR

" *Use every resource you can. At my firm, a résumé coming from someone inside the firm automatically jumps to the top of the list. There are so many qualified people out there and most employers are looking for people who are pleasant and hard working—the best way to learn that quickly is from someone who knows the applicant. Hiring is a pain and any way employers can speed things up and make it easier, they will.* "

   –Law Student, San Diego, CA

The Fact of the Matter

In a study of the 2003 law school class, the National Association of Legal Placement found that students engaged in the following activities during the summer following their first year:

Activity	Percentage of Students (sample 3,467 students)
Did not work or study	1.7%
Summer school and/or study abroad	7.7
Worked only	73.8
Worked and summer school/ study abroad	16.8

For those that did work, the NALP found the following:

Summer Position Held	Percentage of Students (sample 3,141 students)
Paid legal position	57.5%
Volunteer legal position	14.1
Nonlegal position	9.8
Research assistant position	7.5
Work-study position	3.3
Judicial extern	7.2
Type of job not reported	0.6

(Source: National Association of Legal Placement, First Year Summer Activity Survey, 2003)

" *Use upper level law students as a resource for finding out about law firms when you have an interview with one—find out who worked there before and ask them about it.* "
  –Law Student, Boston, MA

Whatever you decide to do during your law school summers, just be certain that you are doing it deliberately. You may choose to study abroad, research, work, or even take additional classes to get ahead. Most voices of experience would suggest that the best bet during law school summers is to line up internships, externships, or clerking opportunities. Even if you are unable to secure a job early on, most firms, companies, nonprofits, and organizations will allow law students to volunteer for experience during the summer months.

CHAPTER 10

Final words of wisdom

> *"Realize that your life is about to dramatically change. The person you were when you entered law school is probably not going to be the same person you are when you finish. Remember how to have fun. If you aren't in the top 20 percent, it's okay. Some days you will lose your mind, just don't lose yourself."*
>
> **–Lawyer–Legal Malpractice Law, Sacramento, CA**

This chapter is one last chance for the Voices of Experience to share their final pieces of advice with you. While this chapter provides closure for this book, if there is one message that is consistent across the recommendations, it is that it should not be the last word on your law school experience. Law school will be challenging, but it is doable and you will come out of it changed for the better. Good luck with your endeavor—we look forward to welcoming you as a fellow lawyer!

AVOID COMMON PITFALLS

"Don't compare yourself to anyone else; you'll hear people saying they're done with their outlines or they've read weeks ahead and it's either not true or they just study differently. Do what works for you. What would I have done differently? I would've stayed up-to-date with my reading in all my classes, especially bar courses. It doesn't take more than a few minutes every day. I would've liked to participate in the clinic."
–Law Student, Los Angeles, CA

"*I worked throughout law school to make ends meet. Don't allow any commitments to come between yourself and studying during your first year.*"

–Lawyer–Business Law, Alexandria, VA

"*If you work hard, you can still have free time. Use your time efficiently. It's not the quantity of work you do, it's the quality.*"

–Lawyer–Civil Rights Law, San Francisco, CA

"*If you were a good student all your life, just keep doing what you have been doing, and you will do great. Do the reading. Do your own outlines. You can use old outlines as guides, but do the reading and doing your own outlines will place you at the top of your class.*"

–Law Student, San Francisco, CA

"*Fear of failure is your greatest asset in law school!*"

–Law Student, Chicago, IL

"*If there is one thing I wish I would have done differently my first year, it would have been to focus my studies more on memorizing the black letter law and practicing application (through practice tests and questions in commercial outlines). Remember that class participation is little (if any) of what determines your grade, and that grades make more difference than just about anything else in landing a big firm or competitive government job.*"

–Law Student, Chicago, IL

"*Don't listen to what other 1Ls tell you about grades, studying, etc. Everyone is different and law school is a unique experience for us all. Make the best of it by staying true to yourself, your personality, and your way of thinking, and study in the way that works best for you and you will do fine.*"

–Law Student, Dallas, TX

" *I used a combination of reviewing my handwritten notes, flash cards, and practice exams to achieve my good grades. If you try to 'cram' like a lot of students do as undergrads, you are setting yourself up for a lower grade. The professors are not looking for an outline on the exam, but rather, your analysis!* "

   –Lawyer–Environmental Law, Byron, IL

" *Don't be the type of law student who lies or exaggerates about your studying, job prospects, etc. Things like that only give people more reason to not like lawyers!* "

   –Lawyer–Trusts and Estates, Boulder City, NV

"*Never ever discuss an examination after it's done. Everyone else is as worried, frustrated, and tired as you even if they act like nothing is bothering them. Make friends fast and attack studies together. Do not assume that you have any greater intelligence or aptitude than your fellow classmates. You are all in the same boat now and should be there to support each other over compete with each other. Answering something wrong in class and having the professor mock you is a rite of passage and it will happen to everyone. Do not feel embarrassed when it happens to you and do not mock or laugh at others when it happens to them. Brace yourself; it will be a wild (and ultimately worthwhile) endeavor.*"

–Lawyer–Civil Rights Law, Greensboro, NC

"*Use the table of contents from your book, and fill each topic with notes from class. This is a great way to jump start your final outline.*"
   –Law Student, Philadelphia, PA

"*Doing well on the test has less to do with having a comprehensive knowledge of the law, and more to do with the procedure of test taking. That aspect took me by surprise.*"
   –Lawyer–Litigation, Warwick, RI

LEARN FROM OTHERS

"*Have someone help you understand what it takes to do well. I'm not talking about a lecture or a class. Have someone who went through it explain the outlining process, how to pull out important pieces of information, and how to process and remember all the information. For those of us that did not have a liberal arts undergraduate education, it took a while to learn this process.*"
   –Law Student, Miami, FL

"*Talk to people who have been through law school to try and get an idea of different studying techniques people use. Whether it be taking notes on your laptop during class or handwriting your notes or doing outlines or flashcards or study groups, different things help people that first year in different ways. Embrace the advice that everyone has to give you and try different studying techniques.*"

–Lawyer–Mergers and Acquisitions, Chicago, IL

"*I did not take any review courses during law school, only for the bar exam. I was not really made aware of these courses at the time, but if I had taken them, maybe my first-year grades would have been better.*"

–Law Student, Boston, MA

STAY POSITIVE!

"*Stick with it. The closest thing that I can liken 1L to is military boot camp. The instructors are there to break you down and rebuild you. Do not fight it, because 1L is where you learn to analyze problems like a lawyer. If you stick with it, you will thoroughly enjoy the subsequent years.*"
–Lawyer–Real Estate Law, Santa Monica, CA

"*Ignore negative peers. Law school is competitive and it's the insecure students who are always trying to psych out peers. Likewise, just because a student seems to be vocal and confident in the classroom (i.e., being a 'talker'), it's those very same students who, generally speaking, are the ones who do not know what they are talking about and you will realize this by the end of the year. It's important to surround yourself with good people; likewise, align yourself with peers who seem committed to producing a good work product (if you're going to go the study-group route). And, forget about making a fool of yourself—no one cares. Rather, people are too self-involved to realize that you are making an ass of yourself—they're just happy that they are escaping being called on and making an ass of themselves.*"

–Law Student, San Diego, CA

"*I worked full time while going to law school at night. The best thing for me to do was just take it one week at a time and not look at the big picture because it can be very overwhelming. Once I got into a routine, the next three years flew by.*"

–Lawyer–Class Action Law, New York, NY

"Keep a positive attitude and do not worry about grades. Just study really hard and put in the time and the rest will fall into place. If you constantly think about grades, you are not focusing on learning the material, which is the most important concern!"
   –Lawyer–Class Action Law, Highlands Ranch, CO

"Whatever happens, don't give up. The first year of law school is made to sift out those who aren't serious about continuing. It gets a lot better once you understand the law school system."
   –Law Student, Washington, DC

"It's a myth that everyone has a job lined up when they graduate. I do, but the majority of the students from my class don't, and I am at a respected top 100 school."
   –Law Student, Los Angeles, CA

> **“**I believe that if you keep up with the reading all semester, exams won't stress you out and you will do just fine.**”**
>
> **–Lawyer–Real Estate Law, Bedford, TX**

GO THE EXTRA MILE

> **“**It is really imperative that you put any sort of social life, minus those important family/social events that might come up, on hold for a year. It's not fun, and mainly painful, but that first-year performance really places you where you will land for three years, and consequently, where you will land in job placements over the summers while in law school and then when trying to find a job out of law school. Although I did well in my first year, looking back, I often wonder how much better I could have done had I stayed in on some Saturday nights instead of heading out with a lot of the other 1Ls.**”**
>
> **–Law Student, Philadelphia, PA**

" Read the material efficiently. I had to learn how to read all over again when I was a 1L. Learn how to read quickly, but retain the information. Also, final exams as a 1L are not as bad as they seem. Take a deep breath and trust that you know the information. If you put the time in during the semester, it will pay off on the final exam."

–Law Student, Sacramento, CA

" I really learned how to study in 1L. This enabled me to get high grades throughout law school without having to put in as much effort during 2L and 3L. The students who slacked off first year and then tried to make up for it later never did as well as those who really went for broke first year."

–Lawyer–Medical Malpractice, Chicago, IL

"*I don't think just anyone can go to law school. You have to be very dedicated and prepared to work your tail off. Learn how to use Lexis and Westlaw early on in law school because they will become your best friends for various reasons through your law school career. Realize it's okay to stay in both weekend nights while your friends are at the bar because you have over 300 pages to read and brief by Monday.*"

–Law Student, New York, NY

"*I would definitely do most of the work before it comes close to exam period. Outline every weekend the material you cover through the week so you do not get bogged down at the end. Seek tutoring in the beginning and ask questions if you do not understand something. Also, meet with your professors frequently so they know who you are and this sets you apart from other students. Finally, always be prepared for class and participate as much as you can. It makes you learn the material and be prepared for exams.*"

–Law Student, Chicago, IL

KEEP A SENSE OF PERSPECTIVE

" Relax. First year of law school is hard. Things aren't supposed to make sense right away, and if they do, chances are you don't understand them. Take your time, work through the material, and eventually things will make sense. If not, know that most of your classmates don't understand either. That's the beauty of law school: No matter how confused you are, you can find comfort in the fact that everyone else is just as, if not more, confused than you. "

–Lawyer–Elder Law, Ann Arbor, MI

" I was overwhelmed by trying to read and learn every detail. This ultimately hurt me because I got bogged down and behind in all of my reading. If I could do it over again, I would continuously try to boil things down to the essential elements and stay on top of the material, regardless of whether I retained every detail. "

–Lawyer–Class Action Law, Newport Beach, CA

"*It gets very stressful—don't forget to relax every once in a while and remember why you liked your life, your family, and your friends. Reconnect with the good things.*"

–Lawyer–Business Law, Arlington, VA

"*Take deep breaths! It's not hard, it's just a LOT! The first year they scare you to death, the second year they work you to death, and the third year they bore you to death. If you remember to breathe, you'll do just fine. Study smart, study hard, and breathe.*"

–Lawyer–Real Estate Law, Memphis, TN

"*You will never be fully ready. Just know it and accept it, and you will be fine!*"

–Law Student, Dallas, TX

"*The thing to remember is that as much as it seems that everything is a competition (and that's not far from the truth), there is a place for everyone. I adopted the attitude that we were all in it together and complimented my classmates when they handled being cold-called well and commiserated with them when one of our professors was unnecessarily cruel. For me, it was best to adopt a 'we're in it together' mentality, because with so many things (grades, jobs, law review) seemingly out of our control, the only thing we could control was our attitudes with each other. That's just me though. I would encourage first-year students to adopt the approach that works for them. And, oh yeah, those who worked hardest and longest did seem to do the best. So do your own cost-benefit analysis to determine how hard and how long you are willing to work.*"

–Lawyer–Legal Malpractice Law, Superior, WI

"*Don't sweat the small stuff. Review general outlines on subject matter before and after class lectures/discussions on that same subject matter. Try and see the big picture and how your first-year courses relate to each other rather than focusing solely on memorizing minutia such as the Rule in Shelley's Case. Find the common themes running throughout the law. Realize that real-world problems often go back to the cases learned in the first day of each of your core areas.*"

–Law Student, Washington, DC

"*I was surprised how much I enjoyed law school after all the scary books out there on the market tell you otherwise.*"

–Law Student, New York, NY

ABCs of Success in Law School

You are setting into the next phase of your professional life. Congratulations! Law school is not a task but, instead, a challenging adventure. Approach it that way and you will enjoy it a great deal more! Never in your life will you pack so much learning into a three-year period. Whether you take up the practice of law or settle into a different profession to post–law school, you will graduate with an education and experience that will serve you well in all aspects of life! Good luck, and here are the ABCs of success in law school.

"All it takes is hard work."
   —Law Student, Chicago, IL

"Be focused, study hard. Do not get discouraged. Definitely study your outlines closely."
   —Law Student, Los Angeles, CA

"Calm down!"
   —Lawyer–Litigation, Washington, DC

"Do the work you're supposed to be doing starting in your first year and maintain that level of discipline for all three years. This means brief your cases, outline your notes right after class, obtain past exams, and do practice questions. This is really the ONLY way to not just get good grades but to really learn the material. The more you learn during law school, the less stressed out you'll be when studying for the bar exam. Get into the habit early so that you'll be prepared in the end."
   —Lawyer–Business Law, Baltimore, MD

"*Enjoy it while you can; it goes by too fast. It is not life or death; stress less, learn more.*"
–Law Student, Denver, CO

"*Fight the urge to pull all-nighters. You need time to process and reflect on the material in a well-rested manner.*"
–Lawyer–Litigation, Chesapeake, VA

"*Get ready for a tough year! It was one of the hardest things I had ever done. However, it's a very satisfying achievement to get through it.*"
–Lawyer–Trial Law, Washington, DC

"*Have good organizational skills, and always be prepared. However, the experience is not as tough when looking back on things, so don't be frustrated or agitated by the experience; the material is not that difficult and you will succeed if you put in the work.*"
–Law Student, Miami, FL

"*It's really not that different. If you worked hard in undergrad, you'll work hard in law school. Law school isn't rocket science. Go to class. Pay attention. Take notes. Study for your exams and do practice exams. You'll do fine!*"

–Lawyer–Civil Rights Law, Salinas, CA

"*Just do your homework and keep your life balanced.*"

–Lawyer–Real Estate Law, Scottsdale, AZ

"*Keep up with your reading and try to get to know other students and study with them—it is reassuring to know you are on the same page as others, and it is easier to talk in class if you are used to discussing your assignments with others.*"

–Law Student, Chicago, IL

"*Law school is a marathon not a sprint. Don't burn out!*"

–Lawyer–Product Liability Law, Richmond, VA

"*Map out a plan for your days. Schedule blocks of time for all the various activities and tasks that you must accomplish. Check them off as they are completed. This will help keep you accountable.*"

–Lawyer–Trusts and Estates, Porter Ranch, CA

"*Network, network, network!*"

–Law Student, San Francisco, CA

"*Outline early. Read as much of the assigned material as you can.*"

–Lawyer–Entertainment, Fort Wayne, IN

"**P**art of the battle is knowing what questions to ask professors and lawyers with whom you may work. The way to figure out the questions to ask is to be flexible, stay focused, and treat your first-year course study as if you are representing parties on both sides of the issue."

–Lawyer–Mergers and Acquisitions, Atlanta, GA

"**Q**uestion so you can learn."

–Law Student, Boston, MA

"**R**each out for help when you need it."

–Lawyer–Bankruptcy Law, Chicago, IL

"**S**tay at school to study. You'll get more done than going home and you'll be more likely to meet other students who will become your friends and study partners."

–Lawyer–Trusts and Estates, Edmond, OK

"Take as many timed practice exams as possible."

 –Law Student, New York, NY

"Use commercial outlines to supplement the class lectures. This will be a huge advantage. Commercial outlines really provide a valuable and concise overview of the law."

 –Lawyer–Real Estate Law, Plantation, FL

"Vital to not fall behind in law school. Keep pace with the assignments."

 –Law Student, Houston, TX

"Work as hard as you can the first semester to establish a GPA that can take hits during the rest of the career and still be high.**"**
   –Lawyer–Civil Rights Law, Pittsburgh, PA

"eX**ercise!"**
   –Law Student, Philadelphia, PA

"You will do much better if you settle into law school gradually, sleep every night, and don't sweat the small stuff. Don't leave your common sense at the door; it is very useful.**"**
   –Law Student, Baltimore, MD

"Zero in more on substantive black letter law than case law.**"**
   –Lawyer–Bankruptcy Law, Sacramento, CA